PHENOMENOLOGY

CASCADE COMPANIONS

The Christian theological tradition provides an embarrassment of riches: from Scripture to modern scholarship, we are blessed with a vast and complex theological inheritance. And yet this feast of traditional riches is too frequently inaccessible to the general reader.

The Cascade Companions series addresses the challenge by publishing books that combine academic rigor with broad appeal and readability. They aim to introduce nonspecialist readers to that vital storehouse of authors, documents, themes, histories, arguments, and movements that comprise this heritage with brief yet compelling volumes.

RECENT TITLES IN THIS SERIES:

Feminism and Christianity by Caryn D. Griswold
Angels, Worms, and Bogeys by Michelle A. Clifton-Soderstrom
Christianity and Politics by C. C. Pecknold
A Way to Scholasticism by Peter S. Dillard
Theological Theodicy by Daniel Castelo
The Letter to the Hebrews in Social-Scientific Perspective
   by David A. deSilva
Basil of Caesarea by Andrew Radde-Galwitz
A Guide to St. Symeon the New Theologian by Hannah Hunt
Reading John by Christopher W. Skinner
Forgiveness by Anthony Bash
Jacob Arminius by Rustin Brian
The Rule of Faith: A Guide by Everett Ferguson
Jeremiah: Prophet Like Moses by Jack Lundbom
Richard Hooker: A Companion to His Life and Work by W. Bradford Littlejohn
Scripture's Knowing: A Companion to Biblical Epistemology by Dru Johnson
John Calvin by Donald McKim
Rudolf Bultmann: A Companion to His Theology by David Congdon
The U.S. Immigration Crisis: Toward an Ethics of Place
   by Miguel A. De La Torre
Theologia Crucis: A Companion to the Theology of the Cross
   by Robert Cady Saler
Theology and Science Fiction by James F. McGrath
Virtue: An Introduction to Theory and Practice by Olli-Pekka Vainio
Approaching Job by Andrew Zack Lewis
Reading Kierkegaard I: Fear and Trembling by Paul Martens
Deuteronomy: Law and Covenant by Jack R. Lundbom
The Becoming of God: Process Theology, Philosophy, and Multireligious Engagement by Roland Faber

PHENOMENOLOGY

*A Basic Introduction
in the Light of Jesus Christ*

DONALD WALLENFANG

CASCADE *Books* • Eugene, Oregon

PHENOMENOLOGY
A Basic Introduction in the Light of Jesus Christ

Cascade Companions

Copyright © 2019 Donald Wallenfang. All rights reserved. Except for brief quotations in critical publications or reviews, no part of this book may be reproduced in any manner without prior written permission from the publisher. Write: Permissions, Wipf and Stock Publishers, 199 W. 8th Ave., Suite 3, Eugene, OR 97401.

Cascade Books
An Imprint of Wipf and Stock Publishers
199 W. 8th Ave., Suite 3
Eugene, OR 97401

www.wipfandstock.com

PAPERBACK ISBN: 978-1-5326-4353-8
HARDCOVER ISBN: 978-1-5326-4354-5
EBOOK ISBN: 978-1-5326-4355-2

Cataloguing-in-Publication data:

Names: Wallenfang, Donald, author.

Title: Phenomenology : a basic introduction in the light of Jesus Christ / by Donald Wallenfang.

Description: Eugene, OR : Cascade Books, 2019 | Series: Cascade Companions | Includes index.

Identifiers: ISBN 978-1-5326-4353-8 (paperback) | ISBN 978-1-5326-4354-5 (hardcover) | ISBN 978-1-5326-4355-2 (ebook)

Subjects: LCSH: Phenomenological theology. | Phenomenology.

Classification: B829.5 .W36 2019 (paperback) | B829.5 .W36 (ebook)

Manufactured in the U.S.A.   09/09/19

Scripture texts in this work are taken from the New American Bible, revised edition © 2010, 1991, 1986, 1970 Confraternity of Christian Doctrine, Washington, D.C. and are used by permission of the copyright owner. All Rights Reserved. No part of the New American Bible may be reproduced in any form without permission in writing from the copyright owner.

To Jean-Luc Marion, the Master

The beginning of wisdom is: get wisdom;
whatever else you get, get understanding.

Extol her, and she will exalt you;
she will bring you honors if you embrace her;

she will put on your head a graceful diadem;
a glorious crown she will bestow on you . . .

Hold fast to instruction, never let it go;
keep it, for it is your life.

PROVERBS 4:7–9, 13

CONTENTS

Introduction • ix

1 The Natural Attitude • 1
2 Givenness • 21
3 Interpretation • 44
4 Paradox • 73
5 Ethics • 101

Index • 129

INTRODUCTION

> Be patient toward all that is unsolved in your heart and try to love the questions themselves, like locked rooms and like books that are now written in a very foreign tongue. Do not now seek the answers, which cannot be given you because you would not be able to live them. And the point is, to live everything. Live the questions now. Perhaps you will then gradually, without noticing it, live along some distant day into the answer.
>
> Rainer Maria Rilke, *Letters to a Young Poet*, Letter Three, April 23, 1903

OURS IS AN AGE of pollution. Light pollution. Noise pollution. Chemical pollution. Digital pollution. Dietary pollution. Saturated by a host of things that lack substance, we sense a deep malaise within our souls. We are saturated, yet not saturated; feeling, yet not feeling; yearning, yet not yearning; loving, yet not loving. We have lost sight of the stars. We have lost sound of the birds. We have lost taste of the elemental. We have lost smell of the flowers. We have lost touch of the human. We have forgotten who we really are because we have forgotten the most important questions.

The question of God has become incidental to existence, even though it remains bound up with existence. The question of love is left alone because of the numbness unfelt in the wake of pain. The question of meaning lacks meaning because meaning has been trampled beneath meanness. Instead of asking the question why, we ask what we think to be more grown-up questions: how much, how little, who will notice, who cares? Personalized humanity has given way to impersonalized economics. Personalized work has given way to impersonalized machines. Personalized intelligence has given way to impersonalized artificial intelligence. We seem to be trending in directions that are devastating in the long run, even though some of us meanwhile enjoy short-term gains. We undoubtedly have a problem.

So there is a laundry list of symptoms, but what is at the root of it all? We do not ask why enough. We do not contend for meaning enough. We do not deny ourselves enough. In a word, we do not contemplate. To contemplate means to ask why a lot. It means to wander and to wonder. It means to seek in order to discover. It means to foster virtue according to the demands of truth and responsibility. To contemplate requires that I devote myself to love because clearly there is no greater enterprise. It requires that I think along an ever-expanding horizon. It requires that I search as far as the margins of the universe even if these margins exceed my physical or intellectual grasp. Contemplation prevents us from confusing the part for the whole, the self for the other, the human for the divine. Contemplation aims at calling a thing what it is rather than calling a thing what it is not. Contemplation gropes for the essential—that which is at the heart of what we call reality.

Introduction

But how can I begin to contemplate if I never have been taught? That is precisely the purpose of this book: to cultivate contemplation. Never has there been a time in history when the practice of contemplation within popular culture was on the verge of extinction like it is in our own. In times past, nature guided people in contemplation as within a monastic womb of wakefulness. Today, however, we have infiltrated the beauty of the natural order with our technological ugliness: cold metal; obstinate cement; obsequious cables, cords, and lines; angry engines; and towering antennae. Since it is impossible to start over or to uninvent all that has obscured the glory of the natural world, we must learn to contemplate in spite of our incontemplative inventions.

We are in need of a method and the good news is that there is one nearby. It is called phenomenology. Inaugurated officially by the German mathematician-turned-philosopher Edmund Husserl (1859–1938), phenomenology is a step-by-step approach to the most certain and clear data of human experience. Phenomenology is a science. In fact, phenomenology is the science of science because it is the science of experience—any and all experience. And what is the content of our experiences if not phenomena? Every experience is filled with phenomena. Phenomenology is the science of phenomena. From its Greek origin, *phainómeno* ("that which appears or shows itself"), a phenomenon means anything and everything experienced by conscious perception, including consciousness itself. A phenomenon is what gives or signifies itself within experience. A phenomenon could be anything perceived by the senses—an image, a sound, a texture, an aroma, a taste, a concept, an idea, a memory—but, most of all, a phenomenon is any meaning or signification intuited consciously. What phenomenology observes and measures is meaning.

It is the science of meaning. It gathers up all meanings given or signified within experience and describes them through the process of interpretation. For the science of phenomenology, phenomena themselves are its data (*datus* "giving," *datare* "to keep giving") because they give themselves to perception.

Phenomenology aims to get at the *lógos* of logic and the *ratio* of reason. It peels back the onion, so to speak, to investigate what is at its core without discarding any part of the onion. It takes all into account. It interprets generously and describes sincerely, dissecting and interpreting the very process of interpretation. It avoids pretension because it unmasks all pretension by the power of its humility. Phenomenology is a humble approach because it does not rule anything out-of-bounds from the start. It does not disregard any experience as unworthy of attention. Rather, and above all, phenomenology is the science of possibility. For this reason it is the best science because it suspends all judgment before conducting the experiment. It does not rule out possibility but awaits its revelation.

Phenomenology is a lot like jazz music. It has some set chord changes and tunes but the rest is open to creative improvisation. Phenomena work this way. They give themselves, and most often we have no control over what they give. Meanings crash upon us from every direction much like inspiration fills a jazz musician while performing a new solo. Phenomenology also is a lot like sports. Why do sports never grow old? It is because no one knows in advance exactly what will happen through the course of the contest. Sure, we may bring our predictions and expectations, but the truth is that sporting events are filled with surprise. And so we play or watch yet another matchup. In a similar way, phenomenology does not like things such as weather reports, fortune-telling, calendars or immovably set schedules. It operates on its own time that is much different than that measured in equal increments. Oftentimes forecasts can be wrong or incomplete. Calendars, too, can limit our imagination of the meanings of time. And perhaps the goodness of the future is that it is not meant to be known in advance like watching a rerun episode in which the outcome is assumed. Phenomenology resists the perception of life to be dominated by predictions. Instead, phenomenology clears a space for the purity of passive perception to receive phenomena that give themselves by themselves, according to their own jurisdiction and authority.

It is important to note that phenomenology is not a set of strict doctrines but a toolbox or an atrium. Phenomenology has no systematic canonical presentation in its history. By its very nature, phenomenology is elusive to define, evasive to pin down, and fugitive to control. It is mystical rather than mundane, loquacious rather than laconic, voluminous rather than virulent. It insists on saying something in five hundred words when it could say it in only fifty. Phenomenology is as unpredictable as it is unsuspecting. It is coy because it is contemplative. These are some of the reasons why phenomenology remains largely inaccessible to so many people today. In the pages that follow, I hope to liberate phenomenology from its infelicitous seclusion from the public arena.

To this end, the book is composed of only five short chapters. Each chapter features one of the most primary terms of phenomenology in order to access its meaning better. Chapter 1 begins with the first step of the method: bracketing the natural attitude. Phenomenology begins with a conversion experience—an ongoing conversion experience—and chapter 1 seeks to ignite this conversion. Chapter 2 follows with the fruit of conversion: the concept of givenness. Givenness is the centerpiece of phenomenology, as it refers precisely to the data of this science of science. Chapter 3 attends to all that envelops every instance of givenness, namely, the layers of interpretation that accompany every datum of givenness. Not only does phenomenology describe what gives, it also describes how it gives through the careful process of interpretation. Chapter 4 considers the phenomenon of paradox as a privileged phenomenon in the way possibility emerges from alleged impossibility. As the science of possibility, phenomenology is interested especially in those phenomena that give more than meets the eye. To round out the book, chapter 5 will touch on the ethical implications of phenomenology. It will ask how the phenomenologist is inspired to live as a result of fruitful contemplation of givenness. Altogether the reader will leave with a basic and summative understanding of phenomenology, even if only a novice's introduction.

In pursuit of its goal, this book will take the reader on a tour of the method of phenomenology with constant reference to the life and teachings of Jesus of Nazareth. Why? It is because the author is convinced that the fullness of the method is found in its passage from exclusive philosophy (reason alone) to the unlimited vistas of theology (divine revelation). If phenomenology is committed to protecting the rights of possibility, it cannot stop short of the possibilities of divinity and the self-revelation of this divinity. In other words, the most rational science is the one that remains ever open before the data that give themselves within experience, even within religious experience. Meaning means no matter where and how it means.

Inevitably this book will offend the sensibilities and pretensions of many experts in the field of phenomenology. Yet it is at the expense of these minor offenses that this book is directed toward a more public audience. Working to overcome the divide between the academic elite and the general public, this book intentionally sacrifices scholarly rigor and nuance for a basic introduction to phenomenology as a method that anyone could use in daily life. To this end, I will refrain from excessive name-dropping and footnotes altogether. I will not quote or reference any other authors at length in order to keep the text as readable and accessible as possible. For a much more precise account of phenomenology as it has evolved over the past century, I refer the reader to my 2017 book, *Dialectical Anatomy of the Eucharist: An Étude in Phenomenology*.

Some readers may object further that including so many references to the life and teachings of Jesus of Nazareth is unwarranted and unhelpful for a book that would introduce a method that is originally philosophical and not theological. This is a valid objection and, again, I would like to make the case that (1) phenomenology reaches its full scope and potential in its use within theology, and (2) because many readers will be familiar with Jesus to a high degree, reference to him will animate what otherwise might be a dry and sterile text on philosophical methodology. My hope is to assist the inculturation of the gospel into the soil of phenomenology and, in turn, to depend on phenomenology to help inculturate the gospel into the pervasive secular and materialist worldview that spreads around the globe like a sweet and oblivious toxin.

Finally, I write under the conviction that Jesus of Nazareth is the greatest phenomenologist in history because he lived it. Even more, if theological assent is granted to the claim that Jesus is the eternal God in the flesh, then Jesus signifies the possibility of the impossible inasmuch as the concept of God includes all possibility by definition, even the impossibility of impossibility (see Matt 19:26). Yes, the testimonies surrounding the life of Jesus are replete with stories of miracles and messages of invincible hope—above all, the proclamation of resurrection from the dead! Yet would this not be the greatest possibility for a science of the possible? Would this not be the most interesting and valuable datum within human experience? If so, why would phenomenology not investigate such data, even if accessible primarily by way of testimony? After all, what data do not come to us by way of a multitude of testimonies and interpretations, even those of our five physical senses?

Phenomenology: A Basic Introduction in the Light of Jesus Christ invites us to allow the life of Christ to illuminate our perception. Without such personal illumination, perhaps we may tell ourselves only what we want to hear instead of hearkening to the voice of the other who summons us to the heights of the possible. In the end, phenomenology refers to a life governed by encounters with otherness—a paradigm shift in which I realize that I am not at the center of the universe once again. Phenomenology teaches us to give priority to the given because it gives us to ourselves in each and every encounter. This is not a contemporary Gnosticism because it will be argued that phenomenology leads us to encounter with the person, Jesus Christ, and not the other way around. The gospel of Jesus is not so much a set of doctrines, an ideology, or an assemblage of esoteric abstractions. Rather, the gospel of Jesus has to do with love who has a face and a name that is manifest in visible flesh and proclaimed in invisible voice.

Donald Lee Wallenfang, OCDS
Emmanuel Mary of the Cross
The Feast of Our Lady of Mount Carmel
July 16, 2018

1

THE NATURAL ATTITUDE

AS ITS NAME SUGGESTS, phenomenology investigates phenomena—any and all phenomena. A phenomenon is anything that happens, signifies, or shows itself within human experience. Phenomena are the stuff of experience. Experience is built by phenomena. Every experience consists of an encounter between the person who does the experiencing, the phenomenon that is experienced, and the interaction between the two. Let us consider an example. I am walking outside on a sunny day and all of a sudden I hear a buzzing sound near my ear. The sound is more pronounced in kind, so I begin to wonder what kind of insect is flying at my ear. Many phenomena ensue: seeing that the insect is a honey bee, feeling slight fear that I may be stung, and all of the associated meanings that accompany the present experience.

The beauty of phenomenology is that it never is finished in its investigation and description of an experience. Because it is open-ended and led by possibility, phenomenology follows one meaning to another. Buzzing sound. Sight of honey bee. Motion. Fear. Distance. Honey. Sweet. Flowers. Colony. Hive. Pollen. Queen bee. And the description continues. This is the beginning of contemplation. This is how contemplation works. Contemplation embarks on discovering a cornucopia of meaning and meaningfulness. Meanings are plentiful and phenomenology helps promote the virtuous habit of contemplation.

I. THE NATURAL ATTITUDE

There is one arch-nemesis opposed to good phenomenology and fruitful contemplation. It is called the natural attitude. What is the natural attitude? It is a biased attitude. It is a worldview calcified by assumptions of all sorts. It is an outlook that is colored by past experiences that form the rules for present experience. A person living according to the natural attitude is accustomed to saying things like, "That could never happen. That is impossible. There is nothing new under the sun. There is no God." A person living according to the natural attitude has silenced certain questions because they do not appear to be financially or socially profitable. The natural attitude passes judgment prematurely and does not give new (or old as new) ideas or experiences a chance. The natural attitude closes the door on possibility because it is convinced that it already knows what is.

The problem with the natural attitude is that it is not fair to the data of experience. Instead of gathering data as they give themselves within experience, the natural attitude assigns the terms and conditions of what may or may not give itself in advance. The natural attitude prevents phenomena from giving themselves as they may. It limits the possibilities within experience by imposing unwarranted qualifications for phenomena to earn the right of their own appearance.

Yet this is not even how our five senses work. Our eyes and ears do not determine the parameters of what they receive. They simply receive. Our nose and tongue do not assign the qualities of the aromas and tastes they perceive. They simply suffer them. Our bodies do not designate the characteristics of phenomena they encounter. They simply undergo them. Our bodies and senses are radically passive media in relation to the world. Though I can respond with some level of agency to phenomena as I encounter them, I do not invent phenomena as they give themselves to me. In this way I am their servant and not their master. I am their accomplice and not their manufacturer. I am their depot and not their dispatcher.

The natural attitude is the first and recurring opponent to overcome for the method of phenomenology. Without unmasking this formidable foe, phenomenology cannot begin its task of passive receptivity to what gives itself within experience. Therefore phenomenology always is beginning. It begins with a conversion away from the natural attitude and toward what gives. This conversion must happen daily, even at every instant so as not to hinder what gives itself by itself. In order to ask what gives with absolute openness, the phenomenologist must forfeit the question, what gives not? All biases and presuppositions must be shed as a snake sheds old skin.

II. BRACKETING THE NATURAL ATTITUDE

Once the natural attitude is identified, it must be purified. The first step of naming the natural attitude begins the process of its purification. Similar to the way a physician first must diagnose an ailment in order to treat it, once the natural attitude is diagnosed properly, including its level of severity within a person, it is ready to be deconstructed and set aside. Phenomenology calls this process of purifying the natural attitude bracketing, also known as the phenomenological reduction. From the Greek word *epoché* ("to stop, cease, suspend, pause"), intentionally bracketing the natural attitude involves suspending judgment about a particular phenomenon or possibility. Without suspending the natural attitude, we miss the essences of things. In bracketing the natural attitude, fuller access is given to the phenomenon—to the thing itself that first gives itself to the human subject. Instead of asking, What is it?, phenomenology asks, What gives? For phenomenology, to be or not to be, is not the question after all. Questions about being and existence are set aside when the natural attitude is bracketed. This is done because oftentimes our assumptions about what is interfere with our experience of what gives. Since the natural attitude causes a reductionism within perception, the reductionism must be reduced in order to prevent the phenomenon and all it gives from being reduced.

The natural attitude is bracketed every time we negate the negation of possibility. This means that whenever we assume that something is impossible, the alleged impossibility itself must be rendered impossible, thereby reopening the field of possibility once again. Because the impossibility of impossibility is possibility, every presumed impossibility is a roadblock for the possibility of the self-revelation of phenomena. Judging a phenomenon to be or not to be in advance is like deciding the outcome of an experiment before it is performed. That would be bad science. Similarly, bad phenomenology passes judgment prematurely, before an experience has run its course. The natural attitude is content to put things in neat and tidy categories before giving phenomena a chance to reveal themselves as they may.

The Natural Attitude

Even the fact that we can draw a line between possibility and impossibility suggests the possibility that this (superficial) line can be crossed. Phenomenology reminds us of the possibility of possibility over and over again. This is its genius. This is its great value for daily life. Instead of interpreting our experiences as boring, mundane, ordinary, and monotonous, everything lights up because every phenomenon is a new creation. And this is the truth. It is not merely wishful thinking or naïve blissful ignorance. It is life ever blissful not because of ignorance but because of insomnolence. We sleep not while awake so that we do not miss out on the ceaseless epiphany of living. We refuse to sleepwalk through life so that we do not fail to receive the beauty of the other. We keep watch so that the destination of the gift is fulfilled. We begin to perceive with wonder the incredible meaningfulness of life and develop a hunch that we were made to breathe the drama of the gift.

Oftentimes the natural attitude is subdued by saturated phenomena that befall us outside of our control. These phenomena disorient the disorientation of the natural attitude and, in effect, reorient consciousness around the prerogatives of possibility. Saturated phenomena send us into a tailspin of vertigo that upsets our self-insulated comfort zones and calculated corners of being. Bracketing the natural attitude is spurred on by the grace of saturated phenomena. This is to say that bracketing the natural attitude is difficult to accomplish by one's willpower alone. It depends, largely in part, on the effect saturated phenomena have on a person. For example, if I have become cold and unconvinced by love, as if true love is not possible after all, it will require the love another has for me to persuade me to believe in love again. Love loves love into love. Love, as a saturated phenomenon, rejuvenates the possibility of love. It takes an other-than-the-self to awaken love in the self because love signifies personal gift that registers between persons. It takes two to tango. Because the natural attitude is reinforced by self-interest, self-concern, and non-disinterestedness for manipulating truth into a self-serving caricature, the self must be displaced by the other to restore vigilance of the gift. Evidence of the absence of the natural attitude is the presence of the gift—when all experiences are interpreted according to the play of the gift. For without the interpretive measureless measure of the gift, possibility remains impossible. With the bracketing of impossibility by the saturation of the gift (givenness), possibility becomes possible once again.

III. THE NATURAL ATTITUDE IN EVERYDAY LIFE

Now that the natural attitude and the possibility of its bracketing have been introduced, let us consider an example from everyday life. Phenomenology is done in the first person, that is, it makes its description of a given phenomenon from the direct perspective of the self. It will use the first person pronoun, I, as the primary point of reference. The world gives itself to me, and, even if I refer to the experience of the other through the phenomenon of empathy, I will describe the experience of the other through my own experience. For phenomenology, as the science of meaning, its laboratory is life and every experiment involves first-person description. Let us proceed then to describe a scene from everyday life, taking my own life as the material for our experiment in phenomenology.

Before anything else, I am a husband and father. The meaning of these terms continues to unfold throughout my life. I have six children and at present the youngest is three years old. His name is Oliver. Oliver and I love to walk outside in the woods and look for animals: deer, frogs, toads, snakes, birds and many more. Sometimes we walk side by side. Sometimes we hold hands. Sometimes I give him a shoulder ride. It all depends on our moods, the weather and other factors. How is the natural attitude at play in this kind of experience?

It's been a long day. Many tasks to accomplish at work. Many emails, grading, meetings, teaching, (never enough) writing and the like. I arrive at home later than I had hoped on this beautiful spring day, the temperature hovering around 60 degrees Fahrenheit. I pull up the driveway in my car and there is Oliver waving to me, desperately wanting to tell me about adventures he had that day. I listen without appearing to be distracted by anything, though perhaps feeling a bit disappointed with myself for my lack of productivity, my falling short of my goals for the day, my lack of clarity about who I am and what I'm supposed to be doing, my inability to prevent mild to severe headaches at times. I eventually work my way into the house to put down my bag, change my clothes, grab a snack, and reemerge into the great outdoors with my son. My wife, Megan, asks me to change his diaper and to play with him while she talks with her mother. I feel a great sense of joy in doing so, while still wrestling with so many other things that preoccupy my thoughts and imagination. I know I must detach from the preoccupations, but how?

On this day the natural attitude haunts me according to its arsenal of "more important things." I continue to check my work email on my cell phone every time I walk past the kitchen counter. Am I not finished with my work away from home for the day? The natural attitude tries to convince me that there is nothing new under the sun after all. I will go outside with Oliver, we will walk through the woods and encounter nothing new, nothing original, nothing spectacular. My slight headache will grow from mild to worse, and I may even need to take some pills to ease the pain. Nevertheless Oliver and I embark on a new adventure and at least there is part of me that is anticipating surprise.

We set out on our four-wheeler and he takes the throttle. I hand over the reins of the expedition to him and my natural attitude begins to dissipate. Suddenly off to the right we behold a medium-sized animal dancing through the woods. Its fur is of a reddish-orange hue, with a dab of white on the tip of its tail. The encounter lasts only for seconds until the agile mammal disappears from sight. "It was a fox!" I say to Oliver, and he says "fox" too. We try to track down where the animal went, but to no avail. Etched in my mind as a new memory of elation, I replay the episode again and again.

Oliver leads us down another path and calls me to attention: "Deer!" he says. I had not even seen them standing in the middle of the trail. We gaze on their vulnerable majesty and elegance until they decide to stop gazing at us and trot off in the opposite direction. We would encounter five other deer within minutes as the forest grew in its enchantment and mystery. We turn off the four-wheeler and are enveloped in a symphony of birdsong: incredible variety of melodies performed for whoever has ears to hear.

Oliver grasps my little finger and leads me to walk atop moss-covered cinder blocks stacked row upon row. For a moment I feel as if I'm standing upon the parapet of a castle. We marvel together at the embryonic leaves extending in brilliant green, in contrast to their earthy brown stems. It seems as though a message is being proclaimed all around us and I search further into the meaning of this secret kerygma addressed to all who would heed its silent summons.

The Natural Attitude

Still wrapping his little hand around my finger, Oliver leads me down the cinder block castle onto the cool grass under bare feet. He says to me, "Dad, I won't let you fall." I look at his small face and wonder if he speaks a prophetic promise to care for me in old age and illness. I wonder if I should not be saying that to him, but his words seem even more fitting, even more profound. Meaning and meaningfulness have lit up like the dawn of a new day and the natural attitude has been vanquished . . . for now.

This brief yet saturating experience, my outing with my son, Oliver, serves to illuminate how the natural attitude can give way to an attitude of receptivity, docility, wonder and vulnerability cultivated by phenomenology. I could have described this experience in many ways—how many minutes our adventure lasted, how many meters we traveled, the weather conditions as reported by news media, my home address, the amount of property we own, etc.—but instead I concentrated my description on those meanings that flooded my perception while being with my son. Had I let the natural attitude prevail, I might have missed virtually all of these kinds of meaning. Perhaps I never would have taken leave of my house and exposed myself to the unknown, the unpredictable, the uncanny.

Instead, I hazarded the possibility of encounter with what gives and this made all the difference. A radical conversion of the natural attitude was necessary and it will be necessary tomorrow and the next day and the day after that, into eternity. Is this not the meaning of the concept of eternity—possibility unlimited and, therefore, love unlimited, wonderful personal encounters unlimited that do not collapse into some tasteless and insipid reductionism that would disfigure the chaste good?

For the final sections of each chapter of this book, we will regard Jesus of Nazareth as phenomenologist par excellence. A teaching or scene from the four gospels will be unpacked as a way to show the fruitfulness borne at the intersection of phenomenology and theology. Jesus is someone who, in his life and message, signals the exorbitant wealth of possibilities within the human experience—precisely those possibilities that humanize us "far more than all we ask or imagine" (Eph 3:20). If this book confined itself to presenting phenomenology as a method in philosophy alone, it would fail to explore the method's furthest reaches within the terrain of human experience. A science of meaning and possibility must extend as far as meaning and possibility lead: all the way to eternity, all the way to encounter with the concepts of divinity, all the way to the figures and forms of divine revelation. When speaking about the life and message of Jesus, I will take into account all of the data that are associated with him as mediated by the Catholic tradition within the broader category of Christianity.

IV. THE NATURAL ATTITUDE AND JESUS

If there is one thing that is absent from the life of Jesus, it is the natural attitude. Perhaps this is part of the mysterious reason why he never yielded to sin in his human nature, let alone the impossibility of sinning for his divine nature—impossible inasmuch as sin is an eradication of possibility. If love signifies the possibility of possibility, sin signifies a lack of love and thus a lack of possibility. Yet throughout his life and healing ministry, Jesus points to the God of possibility, the God who makes all things new, the God who loves all the way to redemption. There is an eternal newness about love and about the God who is love. And this is the strength of love: love never tires of loving. The gospel of Jesus is the gospel of love—divine Love in person, Love in the flesh, Love who has a face and a name.

The beginning of this gospel is the call to conversion. Every encounter with Christ involves the possibility of further conversion of the human heart. Turning more and more away from sin and toward the God who is love. The conversion to Christ is at once the conversion to love—to love better, to love more intensely, to love more expansively. Anything that stands in the way of this dilation of love must be overcome. Above all, the ponderous inertia of the self must be surpassed since the self is not the reason for its own being after all.

In the first chapter of the Gospel of Mark (1:14–15) the message of Jesus is summed up according to three primary meanings. Let us consider these in turn so as to relate them to the surmounting of the natural attitude.

A. "This is the time [*kairós*] of fulfillment."

Encountering Jesus begins with timing. It is not chronological time, such as the ticking second hand of a clock, but rather it is kairological time, such as those experiences when time seems to stand still or fly by. The Greek concept of *kairós* refers to the time of encounter or a kind of time not measurable by equal increments. This, too, is the time of phenomenology. Every phenomenon transpires in its own time. In my narrative about my son, Oliver, and me above, chronological time is not of the primary essence of the experience. Measurable time is inconsequential to the more prominent meanings that fluctuate according to their own rhythm and dynamism. By bracketing the natural attitude that tends to be infiltrated with the superficial palindrome concept of chronological time, a time of new discovery is opened. It is the time of nature, the time of music, the time of art, the time of dance, the time of imagination, the time of fellowship, and, above all, the time of love and responsibility.

Jesus signifies a doubly saturating concept of time: *kairós* fulfilled. It is a paradoxical notion of an opening and a filling. It is the time zone from which all other time zones are derived. It is the time of eternity that breaks into the temporal flow of life received from eternity. Every phenomenon is pregnant with the potential to open and fill this eternal time zone according to its systolic and diastolic irregular meter. It is a dialectical tempo inasmuch as it circulates along with the circulation of phenomena manifest and proclaimed. The time signified by Jesus defies every concept we have had of time before the time of this encounter. In it the natural attitude is suspended along with all judgment, tampering, and manipulation. There is no grasping involved in this experience of encounter, only receptivity, passivity, and gratuity.

B. "The kingdom of God is at hand."

The meaning of the kingdom of God and its immanence also is relevant for understanding the happy eclipse of the natural attitude. The kingdom of God is the expansive realm where all things are possible. This does not mean that

The Natural Attitude

anything can be thought, said, or done to no consequence. Instead there are thoughts, words, and deeds that are absent from the kingdom of God because their presence would lack presence, their occurrence would deplete occurrence, their eruption would engender corruption. In a word, sin disfigures and distorts the integrity of the phenomenon, the given, the gift. Sin abbreviates possibility to the point of virtual impossibility, though not pure annihilation. The theological concept of hell signifies possibility abridged to the lowest degree possible without ending in annihilation. What prevents absolute annihilation is the Love that loved the beloved creature into existence and refuses to unlove the beloved out of existence.

There is a monarch of the kingdom of God and it is not me. It is God. Untying the Gordian knot of original sin and the misguided lust to usurp the lordship of the Lord of the universe, the advent of the kingdom of God reopens the possibility of possibility. The divine monarch must risk his life, reputation, and supreme dignity to do this, but he does so nevertheless. To subvert the ungodly secular perception of lordship requires the Lord simply to be himself in a "world [that] did not know him" among "his own people [who] did not accept him" (John 1:10–11). The Lord of the universe does not exercise his divine kingship in relation to his creatures by dominating them, exploiting them, or destroying them. Rather he lives how he has lived from eternity. In relation to his finite subjects he serves them in love. Coinciding with the disposition of phenomenology, the meaning of the kingdom of God is at the service of possibility because for this love all things are possible. The natural attitude must be subverted and transfigured into an attitude of perfect receptivity and servanthood to dwell in this city of God.

C. "Repent, and believe in the gospel."

Encounter with Jesus and his message provokes a decision on the part of the encounterer. It impassions a reaction in the face of truth, gift, and invitation. The haughty person does not recognize this perforation of pride to be the greatest blessing and escape. The arrogant natural attitude insists upon its self-sufficiency and denounces the intimation that the ego left to itself is incomplete. For the sacred Ego ("I am") revealed to Moses in the theophany of the burning bush suggests the full circuit of the self's mission in its relation to and responsibility for the sacred Other. To quote the African proverb: "I am because we are; because we are, therefore, I am." It is because there is a you that there is an I. It is because there is a you and an I that there is the potential of forming a we. The trinitarian structure of subjectivity is accessed by laying down the arms of the natural attitude in order to awaken to the peaceful interlude of contemplation.

The Greek word for repentance, *metánoia*, literally means to have a change of mind or heart. It suggests a radical change involving all of one's being. It implies seeing with new eyes and hearing with new ears. The photographic negative of the healing miracles of Jesus points to the inverse wonder of people who seem to have nothing wrong with their five senses but still cannot see, hear, or perceive the truth about God and what it is to be human. The self-righteous—indeed those under the spell of the natural attitude—"have no need of a physician" (Mark 2:17). They think that absolutely nothing is wrong with them "and yet do not realize that [they] are wretched, pitiable, poor, blind, and naked" (Rev 3:17). For the natural attitude to be alleviated a decisive intervention is demanded.

Conversion of the natural attitude, and moreover conversion of the soul, is accompanied by belief and trust in what gives. The ultimate theological term that signifies what gives is grace (*cháris*). Conversion of the natural attitude means relinquishing the right to control the otherness of the phenomenon. Ignatius of Loyola advised his disciples to perceive God in all things, and the faith that exceeds the natural attitude is defined by Jesus as "accept[ing] the kingdom of God like a child" (Mark 10:15). To believe in the gospel conveys a fundamental trust in the goodness of life because it gives (*es gibt*). The child is the model contemplative because she exhibits this precocious naïveté for receiving all that gives with virginal obedience and amenability. For the child, the natural attitude has not set in because it has not had (chronological) time to calcify. The child lives with an attitude of wonder according to her discalced temperament, for she leads us in removing our shoes before the holiness of the Other. Little bare feet pitter-pattering on the cool green grass remind us that in the beginning was not the natural attitude. And neither will it prevail in the end. The child as contemplative evangelist manifests and proclaims the good news because she believes and knows it to be so.

In order to concentrate our analysis even further, let us continue to follow Jesus, the master phenomenologist, at work. The last section of the chapter will reflect on a crucial scene that is related only once among the four gospels, namely, the narration of an anonymous woman allegedly caught in the act of adultery.

V. JESUS AND THE ADULTEROUS WOMAN

Adultery is terrible. Horrific. Worse than death. It is a grave sin against the truth and integrity of relationships, especially within the most essential relationship by which society holds together: marriage. It is defined as an act of sexual intimacy between a woman or man who is married and another person who is not their husband or wife. It involves physical intimacy, even all the way to sexual intercourse. It is a most serious violation of natural law and divine law, akin to murder, abuse, and suicide. It is murderous, abusive, and suicidal indeed because it tears apart the interpersonal fabric of families, tribes, communities, and nations. It virtually annihilates the bonds of trust and fidelity that secure our peace and basic motivation for joyful living. For Torah, it is an act worthy of the death penalty because the act of adultery itself is synonymous with the death penalty. It ushers in death as surely as bullet or sword.

The ancient Jewish community was acutely aware of the seriousness of adultery. It is treated in the law of Moses, or Torah, several times (see Exod 20:14; Lev 18:20; 20:10; Deut 5:18; 22:22–27). With all patriarchal hegemonic contextual considerations acknowledged and set aside, the penalty for adultery between a married (or even betrothed) woman and a man was capital punishment by stoning (Deut 22:22–24). Both the woman and the man were to be stoned to death, beginning with the stones cast by the witness(es) of their adulterous act.

The story told in chapter 8 of the Gospel of John assumes the force of the seriousness of adultery and positions Jesus and his judgment of the case in direct confrontation with the law of Moses. The natural attitude is prevalent on several levels within the details of the story. Where is the man who presumably was involved in the adulterous affair with the woman? Should he not be brought forward as well? Who witnessed this act of adultery and what circumstances gave them access to it? Is this really an either/or predicament—either guilty death or innocent life for the woman—or is there another possibility that might open?

The Natural Attitude

How would we describe the natural attitude at work in this scene? First, it is at work in the lustful intention that brings a person to commit the act of adultery. Jesus teaches of this lustful, or covetous, intentionality elsewhere in the gospels: "Everyone who looks at a woman with lust has already committed adultery with her in his heart" (Matt 5:28). The mortal severity of the sin begins in thought and then is transposed into adulterous gestures, signs, and speech. Lust, as one of the legion of avatars of the natural attitude, diminishes the possibilities of authentic love that is verified by its moral exigencies of fidelity and responsibility. For love without faithfulness and solicitude for the other—for every other—is no love at all.

Second, the natural attitude is on display in the accusers. They want to condemn the woman to death. The fact that she is not called by name suggests the reductionism that has already taken place: reducing her to adulteress, an agent of sin, and that is all. Forgetful of their own personal sins and their inherent kinship with the woman, the bloodlustful men in reality scapegoat their own secretive guilt on this woman who would pose as a replacement sacrifice in perverted reparation for their own shameful thoughts, words, and deeds. They ask Jesus what he thinks ought to be done with the woman, not because they care to consider what he has to say, but as a way "to test him, so that they could have some charge to bring against him" (v. 6). The natural attitude closes itself off to the possibility of being taught and enlightened.

Third, the flipside of the natural attitude of the accusers is just as sinister. When Jesus is left alone with the woman, he does not give absolution for her sins. He simply says that he does not condemn her. The second side of the natural attitude's sword is graceful licentiousness. Jesus's response to the situation is neither condemnation nor approbation.

He does not water down the gravity of the sin but instead calls the woman once again to responsibility: "Go, and from now on do not sin any more" (v. 11). The woman is left to beg forgiveness from her husband, whom she betrayed mortally. What is lacking for the double-edged sword of the natural attitude is love and responsibility. Grace, in the final analysis, does not portray sin as a positive possibility. "All things are possible [*éxesti*], but not all things do good. All things are possible, but not all things edify" (1 Cor 10:23–24). Phenomenology does not imply that all possibilities are equal or that all possibilities lead to further possibility. Rather, phenomenology can describe any and every possibility but in doing so discerns the wheat from the chaff, the true from the false, the authentic from the inauthentic, the virtuous from the vicious, the charitable from the sinful. And it can do this all while suspending a final verdict on a phenomenon.

In this scene in which a woman caught in the act of adultery is presented to Jesus in the temple area, Jesus demonstrates what is meant by the first step of phenomenology: to bracket the natural attitude. His enigmatic writing on the ground with his finger exemplifies this process. Whatever this gesture signifies—for it can signify many things—most certainly it means contemplation. It signifies a disruption of chronological sequence, meter, and expectation. It interrupts with sudden silence the ambiguities of noise and chatter that pollute daily life. By writing on the ground with his finger, Jesus points to something else that nobody recognized. He inscribes something in the sand as a palimpsest that leaves open those unimagined possibilities as a reclaimed future forgotten. Perhaps still left unrecognized by the end of this story, Jesus at least witnesses to an otherwise—an otherwise than predicted, suspected, or planned.

The Natural Attitude

This is phenomenology at its finest: bracketing the natural attitude, attending to what gives, describing what gives, suspending judgment until the time of final judgment. Phenomenology lives within this space of the until. It lives within this in-between time of opening (*kairós*) filled to the point of saturation and abundance. Perhaps this, too, is the meaning of the classic twenty-third Psalm: lacking nothing, verdant green pastures, still waters, restoration of soul, right paths, table set, head anointed with oil, cup overflowing, being pursued by goodness and mercy (as they give themselves!), dwelling in the house of the Lord for endless days. This is the time of eternity, the time prior to Being and beings, the time of the ego's divestment before the good of the other.

Remembering the narrative of the encounter between a woman caught in the act of adultery, her accusers, and Jesus has helped animate, if not incarnate, the concept of the natural attitude and how it can be overcome. This is the first obstacle for phenomenology. Indeed, it is the Goliath within phenomenology that needs to be defeated not by stones of judgment and condemnation but by stones that shatter the "hearts of stone" (see Ezek 11:19; 36:26) that close the door on possibility, especially the most expansive possibilities of love and responsibility for the other who faces me.

The first step of phenomenology has been introduced and commenced. We now are prepared to continue to the next step, which is to contemplate. Chapter 2 will ponder the meaning of meaning by attuning the reader to what gives. Since its beginning, phenomenology has used the language of the given, its giving and givenness to describe most precisely how we experience phenomena. Let us proceed then to a deeper contemplation of the meaning of givenness as the vital centerpiece within the method of phenomenology.

PHENOMENOLOGY

Key chapter concepts: natural attitude, *epoché* (bracketing or suspension of the natural attitude), phenomenological reduction, possibility, *kairós*, kingdom of God, *metánoia*, *es gibt* ("it gives")

DISCUSSION QUESTIONS

1. What is the natural attitude and why is it an obstacle for phenomenology?

2. How does one go about bracketing the natural attitude and ensure that it remains bracketed?

3. Give an example of the natural attitude at work in daily life and the method you would use to bracket it.

4. How does the life of Jesus show an effective bracketing of the natural attitude?

5. What does Christian conversion (*metánoia*) have to do with the bracketing of the natural attitude and how can the latter contribute to the former?

2

GIVENNESS

For phenomenology givenness is everything because everything gives. From the German and French words, *Gegebenheit* and *donation*, givenness refers to the precise nature of any and every phenomenon: it gives (*es gibt*). Every phenomenon gives itself to me. I do not create it or manufacture it. Rather, it gives (*es gibt*). It gives meaning. All meanings, perceptions, and even those meanings we use to interpret phenomena, give themselves to me. This is the very structure of conscious perception. All phenomena crash upon me as data from an elsewhere—even the datum of my own conscious life. The word *datum*, from the Latin words *datare* ("to keep giving") and *datus* ("giving"), means what gives, the given in the equation, the stuff given to conscious perception and observation. All science relies on data and interpretation of data. Phenomenology, as the science of science, examines those data that are most essential and immanent to consciousness. The term *consciousness*, again from its Latin origin, literally means "with knowledge" (*con-scientia*). What do we know if not first what gives itself to us consciously? Phenomenology asks, What are the pure essences of this experience? What gives or signifies in experience are essential meanings of perception and spiritual intuition. Phenomenology attends most of all to the immanent (rather than transcendent) data of givenness or signification within consciousness. The most precise and indubitable data of human experience are these.

Let us consider an example of an experience in order to distinguish between immanent and transcendent data within experience. I am holding a black cat in my arms and petting its fur. It purrs while I pet it and is content to stay rather still in my arms. Transcendent data include everything that I interpret as outside of myself, certainly outside of the domain of my immediate consciousness: the cat "out there," its anatomy and physiology, the sound waves generated from its purring that strike my eardrum and cause it to vibrate, the space that separates the body of the cat from my own body, the color of its fur as it reflects the light of the sun, etc. All of these comprise the data of natural science and can be investigated as manageable external data of sense perception. Yet such transcendent data are only one kind of interpretation that maintains a distance between the perceived and the perceiver. Interpretation according to transcendent (outside-of-the-self) data alone reduces the world to a host of indexed objects that always stand apart from the unacknowledged subjectivity of the ever-hidden neutral observer.

Immanent data, on the other hand, are those I perceive within me—within the spiritual recesses of my interior life called consciousness. These are universal and absolute meanings that give themselves directly to consciousness. They are spiritual essences or intangible eidetic objects for conscious thought: blackness, catness, softness, silkiness, smoothness, delicateness, purringness, whiskerness, toothness, clawness, boneness, eyeness, tailness, felineness, peacefulness, beingness, sedentariness, proximity, docility, relationality, warmness, goodness, stewardship, etc. The description could go on and on. These immanent data are something different than transcendent data, such as the cat "out there" and everything I might assume about the cat and its being as taught to me from "out there." Immanent data give themselves all the way to the degree of conscious intimacy and therefore are indubitable inasmuch as they show or signify themselves absolutely, irreducibly, irrevocably and decisively. Phenomenology deals especially with immanent data because these are the most concentrated, clear and meaningful data of experience. Immanent data exhibit pure and universal givenness, much more so than any data "out there." They form the core of all empirical encounter and lend themselves to the highest levels of contemplation. Phenomenology interprets such data in terms of their givenness to consciousness because givenness most precisely describes the process by which we experience phenomena. Phenomena give themselves to us, and the relationship between the thing/phenomenon in itself and its immanent data given to consciousness are one and the same. For phenomenology, there is no separation between the phenomenon I experience and the thing in itself.

I. GIVENNESS

Givenness is arguably the most exciting concept for phenomenology. It is the prize for the successful bracketing of the natural attitude. As French phenomenologist Jean-Luc Marion has put it: "so much reduction, so much givenness." The more we reduce (or bracket) the natural attitude, the more givenness floods into consciousness. Phenomenology calls the event of givenness entering consciousness intuition. It also designates the process of conscious reception of givenness *noesis*, and that which gives itself to consciousness *noema*. By bracketing the interpretation that would reduce phenomena to what they are, phenomenology lets phenomena reveal themselves according to what they give. Without implying a giver, whether divine or otherwise, phenomenology simply describes the nature of perception: receptivity to what gives. For instance, I encounter brilliant hues of purple, white, gold and green springing from the earth. They give themselves to me as they flutter and bounce at the breath of the wind. They radiate their royal ensemble as response to the light. Ever so delicately they manifest their shape with curves, edges, and perfect proportion. A trinitarian form. They give this way and then that. I survey their noble epiphany from multiple angles. I come near and go far. I look from above and below. I draw close to smell their sweet fragrance and stoop down to trace their concealed origin of growth and vertical extension in spite of the leverage of gravity.

Instead of beginning with the word *flower* or the species of flower, Iris (*Iris sanguinea*, for example), phenomenology begins by describing the meanings that give themselves to perception throughout the experience. Givenness is manifold and it has no beginning or end. It was giving before I perceived its giving and continues to give beyond my rendezvous of perception. Givenness is unconcerned with questions about existence, causality or categories of being. These designations of metaphysics come long after the advent of givenness, the detonation of data. Phenomenology attends to the drama of giving that is constant and saturating. So much givenness is perceived that I only can concentrate the descriptions of my experience on very small portions of all that gives, one at a time. Description itself bears the character of eternity since there is no shortage of meanings that light up for consciousness to perceive, receive, and tell about.

If I began my description with words like plant, flower or Iris, I might miss so much that gives itself in the encounter because I was too hasty in my interpretation and placement of privileged meanings according to culture and custom. While these three terms might be part of the description along the way, phenomenology is careful to bracket categorical reductionism in order to promote phenomenal evangelism. In other words, the faithful phenomenologist is one who lets (*fiat*) give. She lets the phenomenon manifest and proclaim itself, its own meaning and message, its own showing and telling, its own apparition and signification. The phenomenologist in no way wants to infringe on the phenomenon's exclusive right to revelation. Instead the phenomenologist is beneficiary par excellence. And who is the benefactor? The phenomenon and all it gives (*es gibt*).

II. FROM GIVENNESS TO CONTEMPLATION

Instead of living with the natural attitude by which life is experienced like a room with four walls, a floor, a ceiling and no exit, attention to givenness bursts open the superficial boundaries I have assigned to possibility. Imagination is liberated from a distended freedom of artificial possibilities and transfigured toward a boundless freedom of essential possibilities that stem from the genealogy of love. Sofia Cavalletti, biblical scholar and disciple of Maria Montessori, observed how children tend toward "the vital nucleus of things" according to their primary disposition of wonder and awe. In this way children are a model for overly sophisticated adults who have forgotten how to contemplate the cosmos. To recuperate the contemplative gaze of the child by unmasking and deconstructing the natural attitude, adults must seek out once again this vital nucleus of things that communicates itself through its silent gestation of givenness.

Access to givenness—even noisy givenness—demands a conversion to silence and solitude. Consciousness receives the host of givenness through the medium of its ascetic and austere halo of detachment from the all-too-natural attitude. Holiness signifies this departure from the cult of the un-marvelous and a new arrival among the communion of saints who have learned this painstaking art of contemplation. In order for the adult to convert to the contemplative character of the child, he must die. Death is the condition for the possibility of new life. Put to death is the old self of the natural attitude: prideful, lustful, angry, envious, gluttonous, greedy, lazy, vengeful, vicious. Essentially conversion of the natural attitude implies a conversion from sin—a conversion from an egocentric lifestyle to one of solicitous responsibility for the other who faces me. Responsibility opens authentic possibility. Virtue refashions the impotent damages of vice. Love reawakens and sobers up the toxic intoxication of hopelessness and merciless indignation. Conversion of the natural attitude and conversion from sin go hand in hand. So much conversion (reduction), so much givenness. So much givenness, so much contemplation.

Givenness leads to contemplation. How? It takes time to receive and ponder what gives itself. Empathetic receptivity to what gives is nurtured to the measure that I contemplate each and every phenomenon within my experience by asking, What does it mean? On this side of eternity, so many phenomena, so little time. Contemplation loses track of time because time cannot keep track of contemplation. Again, the time of contemplation is immeasurable with numbers or equal increments. For contemplation, not all times are equal. Experience ebbs and flows according to the fluctuating rhythms of what gives. Eternity signifies the time it takes to contemplate. Not a unidirectional endless chronology that would lose interest and become more frightening with the passing of each second. But rather a time zone that dilates with generous expansiveness with every encounter and, above all, upon encountering the face of the other as incommunicably unique and incessantly summoning me to responsibility.

The tradition of Carmelite spirituality, in particular the reform movement of Teresa of Ávila, provides an itinerary for this tremendous vocation to contemplate. There are five traceable steps of contemplative prayer:

1. Vocal prayer
2. Mental prayer
3. Prayer of recollection
4. Prayer of quiet
5. Contemplation or union with God

First, givenness provokes a response from the one who begins this practice of contemplation: at least a verbal utterance of "thank you" or "beautiful" or "so amazing."

For the contemplative these phrases fall off the lips at every turn. This is vocal prayer. Second, the one who dares to contemplate begins as an understudy of mental prayer or meditation. This includes a discursive or roaming rumination on what gives. The word *ruminate* comes from the Latin verb *ruminare* and means "to chew again." Rich foods require chewing. In a similar way rich experiences require rumination—sitting with them and pondering them again and again and again. This is mental prayer.

Third, the soul who contemplates realizes that it has been spread so thin over the course of metered time. This impoverished soul realizes that she is too compromised, too broken to pieces, too fragmented. She realizes that she needs to be gathered together once again, re-membered, re-collected. Her senses have become too attached to virtual stimuli. Her habits have become too mechanized and perfunctory. Her suitors have become too numerous and ambiguous. She knows that she needs to surrender to the One who holds her life and so she enacts—not so much by her own initiative but by the initiative of the One who gives—a movement from activity to passivity at the sway of what gives. Her pieces are put back together because she lets them be reunited. This is the prayer of recollection.

Fourth, the prayer of quiet leads to a hushing of the senses, a quieting of the disquieted appetites that prod the soul in every direction and therefore no direction, a stilling of even intellect, memory, and will that otherwise would remain entangled in some brand of the natural attitude. In radical passivity before what gives, a creative space of mystical experience is elevated and unveiled to the degree that transparency of the soul unfolds. The soul is divested of all pretentiousness, hubris, and duplicity to become an open book before what gives, just as what gives is to be read as an open book for its elected apprentice. This is the prayer of quiet.

Fifth and finally there is the prayer of contemplation, properly so-called, and also described as union with God. The concept of God signifies the utmost in possibility and the very visage and voice of primordial givenness. Because God gives, it gives (*es gibt*). Because of eternal Givenness, givenness gives. Without reducing God to the metaphysical notion of the uncaused Cause (though this idea certainly has a cardinal place in philosophy and theology), God manifests and proclaims Godself on the horizon of givenness precisely as the expansion of the horizon itself. If we took stock of givenness without contemplating the most saturating saturation of givenness, we would break the rules of phenomenology. Yes, phenomenology must go as far as the concept of God because it is this concept that stretches phenomenology to the unbounded recesses of givenness. Givenness guides the soul to contemplation because the stuff of contemplation is givenness. I do not hesitate to call contemplation prayer because prayer is the fruit of conversion away from the natural attitude. One who lives with the natural attitude is rightly called the *insipiens*—the fool who says in his heart, there is no God (see Ps 14:1).

III. GIVENNESS IN EVERYDAY LIFE

In order to access the fruitfulness of givenness for daily living, it is necessary to provide an example of its process of recognition. This process is threefold: (1) bracket the natural attitude, (2) perceive/receive as much givenness as possible, and (3) describe what gives. Let us take the following example of a common phenomenon of nature.

It gives (*es gibt*). Tallness. Height. Exteriority. Roughness. Hardness. Extension. Verticality. Reach. Unfolding.

PHENOMENOLOGY

Opacity. Branch. Foliage. Vessel. Transfer. Leaves. Rustle. Gentleness. Stalwart. Towering. Ascending. Lifting. Raising. Rising. Elevate. Curvature. Erect. Planted. Stretch. Defy gravity. Roots and shoots. Life. Photosynthesis. Reproduction. Seed. Germination. Half hidden, half revealed. Cylindrical. Segmented. Core. Sway. Shade. Needles. Green. Brown. Color. Crevices. Bark. Trunk. Twig. Stick. Wood. Variegation. Bud. Blossom. Dormant. Network. Hollow. Solid. Firm. Dense. Relational. Symbiosis. Biodiversity. Ecosystem. Nests. Fruit. Flowers. Pollen. Stamens. Pistil. Pine cones. Lichen. Burrows. Decay. Death. Uproot. Fall. Succession. Texture. Smooth. Rigid. Sap. Aroma. Perennial. Resilient. Spring. Winding. Drooping. Sagging. Spindle. Straight. Line. Height. Depth. Contrast. Shape. Contour. Silent. Seeping. Growth. Nutrition. Living. Protrusion. Twisting. Grooves. Sapling. Strong. Virile. Gnarly. Sturdy. Fiber. Cellulose. Chloroplasts. Absorption. Excretion. Development. Multivalent. Multifaceted. Organism. Apex. Spread. Bountiful. Plentiful. Beautiful. Good. True. Verifiable. Angle. Length. Maple. Syrup. Sweet. Runny. Flowing. Nature . . .

And so begins a phenomenological description of givenness associated with a phenomenon called tree. Each of the terms above merits patient contemplation. They are not to be read necessarily in sequence and certainly not as quickly as possible. They do not refer to the same type or species of tree, but to several encounters with different kinds of trees. Each concept unfolds a *florilegium* ("gathering of flowers") of concepts. For example, the concept "stretch" unfolds others like: straighten, lengthen, push out, reach, extend, expand, etc. Again, the point is not to define an object once and for all. The point is not to situate a specific being inside a neat and tidy category of being, for example, plant or animal, living or nonliving. Instead phenomenology intentionally brackets and sets aside questions of being in favor of the saturating data of givenness. The description of "tree" above is a beginning and only a beginning. Good phenomenology, much more than encounter with words and pictures on a printed page, involves in-person and in-the-flesh encounters with in-the-flesh phenomena. Responsible phenomenology of a tree necessitates close encounter with a tree: touching it, smelling it, watching it, listening to it, perhaps even tasting it (in the cases of fruit or syrup, for example), and pondering all of the meanings that disclose themselves within the encounter between a tree and me. Phenomenology gathers up the given essences of a phenomenon, not as the nature or ontological category of a being, but as the meanings and significations given by the phenomenon.

Every phenomenon is pregnant with meanings. Every phenomenon bears so much potential to reveal so many meanings to a personal human subject. Humans are the creatures who contemplate. We are the ones who tell stories, narrate our experiences, and do phenomenology. We are creatures of culture, and phenomenology is a method devised to unpack all of the interpersonal meanings that weave together the fabric of culture. This procedure of detecting and describing givenness can be applied to every phenomenon within daily living. Once again, so many phenomena, so little time. Phenomenology slows down the pace of life. It fosters a life at once humble, patient, generous, and merciful. *Despacito*. Slowly, at the pace of a sloth betwixt the branches of life. The most adequate descriptions in phenomenology would be those that are multicultural. Here I write in the English language but a description of a tree involving multiple languages and their respective nuanced meanings would enhance the description and reencounter all the more. Every phenomenon is destined to be inculturated and so give itself in-the-flesh through a diversity of living and incarnate cultures around the world. Every phenomenon is worthy of contemplation because it gives. Whether an ironing board, a garbage can, a speck of dust, or the entire universe, all phenomena have the potential to give rise to further contemplation. Phenomenology gives life to life because life gives life to life. It lives because it gives (*es gibt*).

IV. GIVENNESS AND JESUS

As phenomenologist of phenomenologists, Jesus awakens his disciples to givenness. Subverting social convention and custom, Jesus is accustomed to pointing out the deeper meaning among the most common of experiences. Materials such as water, seeds, fields, money, oil, lamps, salt, cities, bread and wine become media of encounter with divinity. This is precisely the meaning of sacrament. Beginning with the Jewish sensibility that "the heavens proclaim the glory of God" (Ps 19:1), Jesus illuminates the sacramentality of the cosmos. The idea of sacrament opens up a givenness within givenness. Phenomena give more than they give. This is to say that we have the capacity to perceive phenomena as signs pointing to

Givenness

more than themselves. Every instance of matter testifies to the givenness of givenness. Like a Russian matryoshka doll in which each doll serves as the nest of another, every phenomenon delivers itself as a womb of meaning that witnesses to the primordial Possibility that made it possible in the first place.

Jesus's character, as portrayed in the gospel accounts, is one that listens, watches, and notices. In Jesus is revealed a God who stoops down low to listen to his beloved creatures. Reciprocally, Jesus shows that the most direct way to encounter this humble deity is to emulate her humility. Swiss psychologist Carl Jung referred to modern people's incapacity to hear God speak to them. He went on to quote a Jewish rabbi, who observed the problem that people do not bow low enough to perceive God. In the gospels, Jesus exhibits a lifestyle of exorbitant listening. The following excerpt from the Gospel of Luke (12:6, 22–34) showcases the attentiveness of Jesus to what gives beyond measure.

PHENOMENOLOGY

A. "Are not five sparrows sold for two small coins? Yet not one of them has escaped the notice [*enópion*] of God."

The first thing to notice is that Jesus witnesses to a God who notices. His reference to sparrows and small coins suggests that there is nothing that escapes the notice of God. He goes on to say that "even the hairs of your head have all been counted" (Luke 12:7). Notice is the key that unlocks access to givenness. The Greek word *enópion* encompasses the sense of presence—being present to, with, or for another. To say that God takes notice is to say that God is present to what is happening and to the soul who is undergoing some trial or joy. The meaning of notice is to face that which is being noticed—to be met with the otherness of the face of the other. Because God notices, it gives. With the notice of God comes the creation of a creature. In other words, God notices creatures into existence. What phenomenology notices about the notice of God is not so much being, but the act of noticing itself. The phenomenon of noticing is what is noticed by phenomenology. Notice triumphs over the natural attitude that was too busy to be enraptured by the beauty, goodness, and truth of givenness. Ignorance of divine notice is enslavement to the natural attitude.

Detection of givenness begins with taking time to notice what gives itself to perception. Notice looks, listens, loves, and learns. Notice takes note of the notations of givenness. Whereas "knowledge puffs up, love builds up. If anyone supposes he knows something, he does not yet know as he ought to know. But if one loves God, one is known by him" (1 Cor 8:1b–3; see Gal 4:8–9). The idolatry of the natural attitude that claims to know things as totalities is emptied of its hubris by divine notice. When knowledge is converted to love, facts and figures give way to faces and friends. An inversion of the natural attitude takes place whereby my knowledge of phenomena is initiated not by me but by the phenomena that give themselves to me. My knowledge about God, surpassed by my love for God, is authored by God's knowledge of me, or to be exact, God's love for me. The conversion of the natural attitude toward givenness amounts to the inversion of the natural attitude brought about by divine notice.

B. "Notice [*katanoéo*] the ravens . . . notice [*katanoéo*] how the flowers grow . . . Seek [*zetéo*] his kingdom, and these other things will be given [*prostíthemi*] you besides."

In his teaching about radical trust and dependence on divine providence, Jesus charges his listeners to notice the world as God notices it. It is provocative how he does not tell them to notice the Roman emperor, or the grand edifices of the culture, or the accomplishments of athletes or entrepreneurs, or the prowess of the religious elite and most brilliant rabbis of his era. Instead Jesus points to more everyday phenomena: ravens and flowers. Notice. The Greek term *katanoéo* suggests careful observation, pondering and vigilant awareness. It does not mean a fleeting thought or a quick glance. Jesus invites a new thought based on what had been giving itself all along. Stop. Yield. Intersect. First, notice demands a pause in the action. Second, notice yields to what gives itself by itself. Third, notice lets the phenomenon intersect with conscious life, and a generous receptivity to givenness transpires.

Along with the counsel to notice, Jesus exhorts his hearers to seek the kingdom of God with the promise that all will be given within the givenness of this kingdom. The Greek verb *zetéo*, beyond the meaning of seeking, signifies striving for and investigating. An anticipation of surprise is ever present within the pursuit of the kingdom of God.

It is worth investigating without ceasing because all worth derives from the immensity of its givenness: *mysterium magnum fascinans et tremendum*. The meaning of the verb *prostíthemi*, along with the meaning of giving, includes the meanings of addition, increase and perpetuity. Indeed, the gift that keeps on giving into and from eternity. Is this not the most fundamental meaning of the gift: the circulation of eternal love? Givenness attests to the eternity of the gift, eternal love. As Bernard of Clairvaux writes in his eighty-third sermon, "It is true that the creature loves less because she is less [than God]. But if she loves with her whole being, nothing is lacking where everything is given." This is the promise offered along with the kingdom of God: nothing is lacking where everything is given. It gives (*es gibt*) because God gives, and givenness is encountered to the measure that the translucent soul seeks the kingdom of God, like an alabaster jar that pours forth its precious contents accompanied by tears shed in adoration and worship (see Matt 26:7; Mark 14:3; Luke 7:37).

C. "Do not be afraid any longer, little flock, for your Father is pleased to give [*dídomi*] you the kingdom."

Notice of givenness dispels fear because fear is forgetful of givenness and suspicious of forgiveness. The furthest possibility of possibility is forgiveness because it expresses the gift given in advance (for-giveness) and therefore given until the end: "He loved his own in the world and he loved them to the end" (John 13:1b). To put it in somewhat metaphysical terms: givenness gives because forgiveness has given and will give to come. Nothing is lacking where everything is given. The metaphorical signification of God as Father engenders the meaning of perpetual creativity, generation and begetting in the beautiful (*paideía*). Jesus depicts God the Father as delighted to give his kingdom to his beloved children. Fecund givenness unbounded is what is meant by the kingdom of God, especially in terms of personal love and responsibility. Givenness is happening all around us and within us constantly. We have only to notice, receive, and respond.

D. "Sell your belongings and give [*dídomi*] alms . . . For where your treasure [*thesaurós*] is, there also will your heart be."

A most fitting response to the generosity of givenness is the reciprocal generosity of giving away, in a word, responsibility. Jesus rounds out his teaching on the priority of God's kingdom by stressing the vocation to responsibility for the other. Givenness transfigures its recipient into a conduit of its magnanimous conduct. A life-giving metamorphosis takes place by which persons are personalized. Everyone becomes an agent of giving and receiving. Voluntary poverty has meaning not only in the increase of magnanimity and generosity on the part of the giver, but there is something entirely magnanimous about the art of receiving as well. Every beneficiary of gift in turn becomes a giver of gift. Those who give and receive have faces and names, agency and innovation, meaningfulness and purpose. The very meaning of personhood is to be taken up into the drama of the gift. When God gives his kingdom, he gives all; and when God gives all, the only appropriate response of the heir is to give all in turn. Social justice is achieved to the degree that divine givenness is empowered in its witnesses.

In good rabbinic fashion Jesus concludes his teaching with a paradox. One's treasure determines the destiny of one's heart and one's heart determines the identity of one's treasure. The concept *thesaurós* means not only a specific treasure (perhaps among other possible treasures), but the treasury, the treasure house, the storeroom itself. It implies a treasure hunt—recognizing something of exceeding value and searching for it until found. Jesus already has identified this treasure for his audience as the kingdom of God. He speaks elsewhere about the treasure hidden in a field, the lost coin, the pearl of great price, the coming of the bridegroom. Above all, however, he says that "the kingdom of God is among you" (Luke 17:21b). This is to say that the kingdom of God is revealed by the countenance and voice of the other who faces me. Its riches and reward are precisely the fruits of responsibility. Jesus extends the theological ethos of Judaism—responsibility for the other—to its eschatological meaning: heaven is the promised land of responsibility wherein the texture of eternity is determined by my affirmative response to the other who faces me. I sell all I have and give alms not in order to receive some miserable reward on the side of the other, but I do so because this ethical relationship is itself that incomparable treasure that merits an absolute investment. In the end, my heart beats for the sake of the other and because of the Other.

V. MERCIFUL MARIA

Besides Jesus, there is one other who models the perfection of charity, contemplation and responsibility in human history: Mary of Nazareth, mother of Jesus, mother of God (*Theotókos*). In the perfection of the feminine genius, Mary embodies receptivity to gift. She emulates the interior depths of empathy and the exterior reach of solicitude for the other. In the few details we have of her in Scripture and tradition, we have enough from which to weave together a precise recapitulation of the meaning of human. Mary represents the boundless capacities of intuition in how she "kept [*synteréo/diateréo*] all these things, reflecting [*symbállo*] on them in her heart" (Luke 2:19; see Luke 2:51b). That is, all of the phenomena that gave themselves to her, especially that of her son, Jesus, Mary treasured, preserved, remembered and encountered over and over within her heart. This is the essence of contemplation that grants full access to givenness because it lets (*fiat*) give all that gives, above all, that divine Givenness from eternity.

In Mary givenness reaches such a high pitch of receptivity that the impossible gives itself as possible: "for nothing will be impossible [*ouk adynatéo*] for God" (Luke 1:37). The *Logos* of all meaning that gives (God the Son), by the power of the Gift of gifts (God the Holy Spirit) and the will of the Giver of all good gifts (God the Father), becomes flesh from her flesh. As a less-than-ordinary woman, among the *anawim* (poor and meek) of a lowly people of the lowlands (Cana'an), Mary receives her vocation to become the icon and passageway of the Possibility that makes all things possible (see Gen 18:14; Job 42:2; Isa 46:10; Jer 32:17; Matt 17:20; 19:26; Mark 9:23, 10:27; Luke 18:27; Phil 4:13). Humility is the necessary portal for possibility. Mary is hailed as the Immaculate Conception because the natural attitude is not to be found with her, let alone sin. Her moral perfection is achieved by divine initiative and yet confirmed and sealed by her assent at every step. Mary is the one who contemplates givenness to an unmatchable level because she contemplates at the baton of the gift. Mary's contemplation is measured by the immeasurability of love. Her life is pure paradox: virginal mother, married religious, wounded healer, rich poor one, silent speaker, active passivity, agnostic knower, atheistic theist, empathetic martyr, mother of God, supernatural nature. In place of original sin, Mary exhibits unoriginal virtue. The extraordinary is accomplished in the ordinary; the great is manifest in the least; the mega is proclaimed in the micro: "the one who is least [*mikróteros*] among all of you is the one who is the greatest [*mégas*]" (Luke 9:48).

Within the heart of Judaism, a theology of adulthood, Mary introduces a theology of childhood. There is a dual maturity here: that of the adult and that of the child. In Mary is revealed at once love and responsibility, contemplation and ethics, adoration and action. Mary is pictured hardly ever without the child Jesus. Even those icons of her in which the infant Jesus is absent from her arms, it is implied that he is present in her womb, such as in Juan Diego's tilma of Our Lady of Guadalupe. Mary is portrayed as attentive perennially to the life of the child. Where Jesus is, there she is as well. Mary absorbs the world like a child, receiving all that gives with wonder, welcome, and gratitude. Through her feminine genius she relates all that gives to the phenomenon of pregnancy. She witnesses to life as womb and the life that gives itself within the living womb of perception. Mary embodies mercy because the meaning of mercy has its origin in the phenomenon of wombness. Rooted in the biblical terms חֶסֶד (*hesed*), רַחֲמִים (*rahamim*), ἔλεος (*éleos*), and *misericordia*,

Givenness

the word *mercy* connotes several shades of meaning, including kindness, compassion, goodness, piety, fidelity, clemency, forbearance, humility, abundance, godliness, brotherhood, sisterhood, motherly feeling, love. It is revelatory to observe that one of the Hebrew terms for mercy, רַחֲמִים (*rahamim*), is related closely to the Hebrew term for womb, רֶחֶם (*rehem/raham*). This suggests that to be merciful to someone means to care for her as in one's womb. Mary is a living testimony to mercy as she models the resplendent receptivity to givenness.

Mary's visitation to her cousin, Elizabeth, as narrated in the Gospel of Luke (1:39–56), showcases the paradox of adoration and action within the same movement. The name Mary, or Miriam, means "sea of bitterness" or even "drop of the sea," while the name Elizabeth means "God is an oath" or "God is abundance." Bitterness meets sweetness; the drop meets plentitude; the question meets the oath. Two women of witness to two conceptions (one natural, one supernatural) commence a dialogue that is instructive for all humanity. Impregnated givenness within givenness generates new vectors of contemplation and service. With the Christ-child in her womb, Mary has arrived to be at the service of Elizabeth. With the scandalous prophet in her womb, Elizabeth welcomes Mary's helpful company with an unbridled response of praise. A litany of proclaimed blessing fills the air so as to point to the fruitful infant manifest blessings that inhabit their wombs. Visitation becomes contemplation as contemplation becomes visitation. Givenness signals the visitation of the phenomenon, and the most fitting reciprocal response is to embark on a perpetual visitation of the neighbor and even the stranger.

Chapter 2 has probed the concept of givenness around which all phenomenology is oriented. We have observed how bracketing the natural attitude leads to greater access of givenness, and how greater access to givenness leads to contemplation. Finally, we began to sense how contemplation remains incomplete without visitation, that is, the ethical movement toward the other that was initiated by the naked face of the other. Pregnancy was proposed as a paradigmatic instance of givenness concentrated and intensified in all its interpersonal dimensions. Yet we must realize that givenness, or intuition, is only half of the equation of phenomenology. The other half is called intentionality or interpretation. To oversimplify, phenomenology moves in two directions: (*a*) givenness moves toward consciousness (intuition) and (*b*) consciousness moves toward givenness (intentionality) through interpretation. We will leave it to chapter 3 to sketch the concept of interpretation that breathes as the second lung to the concept of givenness.

Key chapter concepts: immanent data, transcendent data, eidetic object, consciousness, intuition, givenness, *noesis*, *noema*, contemplation, notice

Givenness

DISCUSSION QUESTIONS

1. What is meant by "givenness" and why is this concept so central for phenomenology?
2. How does attention to givenness promote contemplation?
3. Perform this experiment: take time to contemplate a given phenomenon and write down all of the data of givenness that you experience.
4. How does divine notice inspire our contemplative attunement to givenness?
5. What do we learn from Mary about merciful contemplation?

3

INTERPRETATION

Up to this point in the book, we have assumed that givenness gives itself to someone. However, we have not taken adequate stock of this someone. Does this someone bring anything to the lived experience (*Erlebnis*) of encounter with givenness? Does the phenomenon itself provide all that is necessary for its reception? Does the phenomenon itself supply all necessary tools for its interpretation? Does the phenomenon interpret itself or does someone else do the interpreting? Chapter 3 will give a description of this integral process of interpretation that happens with the reception of every phenomenon. Phenomenology deflects all worldviews that could be categorized as some type of fundamentalism or ideology. Fundamentalism or ideology refer to a worldview that involves a reductionism of the whole of what gives to only one or some of its parts. Phenomenology avoids fundamentalism, or reductionism, by reducing the reductionism, that is, by bracketing the natural attitude that is constructed by one or another brand of reductionism. Whether political (liberal or conservative), religious, or philosophical ideologies, phenomenology renounces every attempt to dismiss possibility. Even phenomenology could fall prey to fundamentalism within its method: either a fundamentalism of givenness or a fundamentalism of hermeneutics (or interpretation). Holistic phenomenology must allow fair consideration of both what gives and how it is interpreted. Therefore phenomenology is inherently dialectical in nature, including both givenness and interpretation, manifestation and proclamation, contemplation and ethics.

I. INTERPRETATION

The truth of the matter is that whenever I encounter a phenomenon, I bring a matrix of meaning to the experience based on all of my previous experiences. This matrix of meaning is called intentionality. As a human subject who interprets the world I, at the same time, intend the world. I assign meanings to the world I experience in light of previous meanings experienced and remembered. Traditional phenomenology calls this realm of encounter the *Lebenswelt*, or the life-world. My life-world is structured by a developed symbolic order of meanings and significations that I inevitably bring to each and every encounter with a new phenomenon. The challenge for phenomenology is to carry out the reduction of the natural attitude while being careful not to throw out the kernel of givenness with the husk of interpretation. I have no choice but to interpret; however, simultaneously, I have no choice but to uninterpret. In order that I do not steer entirely the phenomenon and its multitude of meanings, I must allow the phenomenon to steer me by letting it take the wheel of experience.

PHENOMENOLOGY

Yet in order not to end up simply floundering in a wordless saturation of givenness, I must maintain some hermeneutic bearings for welcoming the phenomenon as it gives itself by itself. I can describe nothing without language and interpretation, symbol and metaphor, image and concept.

In relation to givenness and intuition, interpreting phenomena is driven by the counterpart concept of intentionality. The intersection between intentionality (interpretation) and intuition (givenness) is where phenomenology happens. In some instances, intentionality meets with a perfect fulfillment of its concept. For example, let us take the common phenomenon of apple. You picture the fruit in your mind, no matter the variety, whether Cameo, McIntosh, Gala, Braeburn, Golden Delicious, Granny Smith, etc. In any and all cases we interpret the apple as a sweet and crunchy fruit, at least within a generous imagination for starters. The concept of apple you have in mind—your intentionality of apple—based on previous experiences of apples meets with the givenness of the intuition of apple, even if there is not an apple sitting in front of you. There is not necessarily an overwhelming response of wonder and awe because the intentionality of concept is filled rather adequately with a manageable and familiar intuition of givenness. We could say that the intuition fills the intentionality like a hand fitting within a glove. This is the case with all so-called objects, or phenomena that we might convert into objects as we receive them. In other instances, however, intentionality either lacks a fulfillment of intuition for its concept or intentionality is saturated by intuition and therefore lacks an adequate concept for the phenomenon that gives itself beyond category and measure.

Interpretation

Let us consider an instance in which intuition is lacking for intentionality. Any abstract idea of mathematics or geometry does this. For example, the equation 2+3=5 involves a comfortable intentionality because it, in effect, dominates the intuition. We are not talking necessarily about five apples or animals or buttons. We are thinking about these numbers in a pure field of abstraction. A simple mathematical equation gives us no cause for consternation because it is rather straightforward and self-explanatory. Intentionality as logical deliberation does virtually all of the work and not much gives in the way of intuition. Numbers, signs and logical coherence make up the abstract intuitions that are altogether lacking in concrete particular content.

In the second case, when intuition overwhelms intentionality, we run out of concepts to situate what gives itself to perception. These cases have been identified as limit-experiences within the tradition of phenomenology. For example, if my father dies of terminal cancer while in the prime of his life, I have no assortment of concepts to come to perfect intellectual terms with what is happening in the face of this tragedy. The givenness of his tragic death saturates my intentional capacity to deal with it. I am unable to manage what is happening according to my intentionality, save for my feeble attempts to tame the experience according to social customs, conventions, and religious rites that seek to reinstate my blessed rage for order. In truth, the event saturates my horizons of intentionality insofar as meaning saturates meaning to the point of a superabundance of meaning or, at the same time, a perceived deficiency of meaning. The saturated phenomenon, as Jean-Luc Marion calls it, accentuates the power of givenness while exposing the limitations of intentionality.

In sum, the three figures of intentionality are (1) intentionality that meets with a relatively adequate correspondence of intuition, as in the case of objects; (2) intentionality that lacks an equivalent reciprocity of intuition, as in the case of abstract formulas, postulates and theorems of mathematics and geometry; and (3) intentionality that is saturated by intuition, as in the case of the limit-experiences of life. It is important to introduce the concept of intentionality with nuance to show that not all phenomena give themselves (or are received) in exactly the same way. Intentionality serves as a kind of conscious canvas upon which phenomena splash with an inscrutable assortment of colors and characters. And sometimes the canvas is unable to handle what gives itself to a saturating degree.

II. FROM INTERPRETATION TO REINTERPRETATION

If the natural attitude involves (hasty) interpretation, bracketing the natural attitude demands (patient) reinterpretation. The nature of interpretation, running reciprocal to the nature of givenness, is boundless and unlimited. Interpretation goes sour when it thinks its work is finished. Just as givenness is never done giving, interpretation is never done receiving. Meanings given are meanings meant

Interpretation

to be received. The Latin roots of the word *interpretation*, *inter-* ("between") *pretius* ("value, price, worth, reward, precious treasure"), suggest an activity that navigates among countless goods, taking inventory of them without ceasing. Interpretation is like the artist who never tires of honing her craft, the naturalist who never tires of exploring nature, the father who never tires of fathering, the lover who never tires of loving. And so the art of interpretation requires revisiting previous interpretations in order to open the floodgates of givenness anew. Not only do phenomena that give themselves to interpretation need to be reinterpreted, but also interpretation itself, as a phenomenon in its own right, needs to be reinterpreted: the interpretation of interpretation of interpretation ... Interpretation is inherently procreative. New meanings arise with each new interpretation or reinterpretation. The repetition of interpretation prevents a closure of givenness and its possibilities.

For phenomenology, interpretation is not so much explanation as it is description. Most scientific explanations aim at telling about cause and effect, identity and difference, being and non-being. Natural sciences, for example, pride themselves on their periodic tables, classifications and genealogies of being. Phenomenology, on the other hand, is concerned with telling about the process of interpretation itself and the most essential data (meanings) that give themselves to be interpreted. In phenomenology the words *interpretation* and *hermeneutics* are used interchangeably. Related to the Greek mythological deity Hermes, hermeneutics includes a mediation and translation of messages of all sorts. Just as Hermes is portrayed as the messenger of the gods by mediating between divinity and humanity, hermeneutics mediates givenness to human intellect by translating embodied perception into language. Even more, just as Hermes has the task of escorting souls to Hades upon death, hermeneutics operates within a realm of perennial ambiguity, attempting to distinguish truth from falsehood in relation to the interstices between that which gives and that which receives.

Because of the lingering ambiguities that envelop every interpretation, reinterpretation is necessary. The interpreter finds himself placed *in medias res* ("in the middle of things") and lacks the privilege of a view from nowhere—positioned neither at the beginning nor at the end of the world and all it gives. Once again, phenomenology calls its practitioners to humility. Similar to how givenness provokes passivity, docility, and obedient receptivity to what gives, hermeneutics fosters conversion of the calloused natural attitude by its perpetual summons to interpret yet again. Both givenness and hermeneutics reinforce the fundamental naïveté that accompanies every new experience. After all, I am not the master of givenness but its attendant. Nevertheless, the filters of language, as a symbolic womb of meaning, await every missionary advance of givenness. Even the term *givenness* demands interpretation along with each and every phenomenon that gives itself by itself. As witness to givenness and its plethora of phenomena and meanings, I can testify to the good news of this givenness only in and through language. For "faith comes by hearing" (Rom 10:17) and givenness must be transposed into word if it is to be communicated at all. And this is precisely the raison d'être of this book: to share the good news of givenness and, moreover, the Givenness who comes to us with face and name and blood and tears, Jesus the Good Shepherd—a message worth reinterpreting at least seventy times seven more times.

III. INTERPRETATION IN EVERYDAY LIFE

In order to give an extended example of the secondary step of interpretation within the method of phenomenology, we must turn once again to the field of the mundane to resuscitate its glory. There are many excerpts of life that we could enlist for our example, such as an event, a text, a gesture, an idea, a song, a work of art, an element of liturgy, the interpersonal relationship, and countless others. For the sake of simplicity and brevity let us choose an event. First, let us recall the threefold process of phenomenology: (1) bracket the natural attitude, (2) perceive/receive as much givenness as possible, and (3) describe what gives. The point of emphasis in this example is the interval between steps two and three, namely, the process of interpreting what gives itself in the experience—interpreting the data of experience and what they mean.

This event involves a visitation. It is not so much that I have chosen this event to use as an example for phenomenology, but it has chosen me. It was not I who went out and visited another person, but someone else came and visited me. In fact, this event involves my own humiliation but a humiliation that is worth revisiting because humiliation is aroused by visitation and, in turn, inspires visitation. Exposure. Nakedness. Vulnerability. Door ajar. Hospitality. Welcome. Intrusion. Disruption. Interruption. Knock. Hello. I must speak. I must listen. Do I empathize? Do I care? Yes, this event begins with a knock on my door, on my office door in the undercroft of the chapel on the campus of Walsh University. I am busy at work as usual, writing a book out of the sense of vocation and the demands of a deadline. The daily liturgy dismisses and I hear the customary din of jubilant voices shuffling just outside my closed (and locked) door. Tucked behind the corner of my office room, I am invisible to those who may happen to pass by the transparent glass panels of my door. Out of sight, out of mind. Unavailable. Do not disturb. I am busy ... for your sake, of course.

On this day something unusual happens. A chorus of the "happy birthday" tune breaks out and I wait to hear whose birthday it is. "Happy birthday, dear Daniel, happy birthday to you!" Daniel. A young man with disabilities, both physical and cognitive. We have had many wonderful interactions before, mostly in and around liturgy. On occasion he serves at the altar during liturgy. I am sure that it would be meaningful if I emerged from my office to wish him a happy birthday and to join in the festivities. Deadlines. Work. I must continue to work. Keep a low profile. I cannot go out right now.

After some time passes the volume of voices decrescendos back to silence. Beautiful, peaceful silence. My work continues in undisturbed silence ... and then there is a knock on my door. You can run but you cannot hide. I look through the glass pane of my office door, and there I see the face of Daniel looking at me. Daniel. A name that means "God is my judge." I make the best effort to smile—to hide the selfish feelings of disappointment that my work is interrupted, that I must depart from my comfortable chair and answer the door, that I must enter into a new conversation of which I am not the master.

A new visitation. Daniel has come to proclaim that today is his birthday, perhaps so that "[his] joy may be complete" (1 John 1:4). For some reason he did not want me to miss out on celebrating his birthday, even if for a fleeting minute of encounter. Not only does he deliver this announcement, he also has come to deliver a piece of cake. He asks if I would like a piece of the remnant of his birthday cake. How could I refuse? Yes, I say, and I receive the cake with gratitude. His widowed mother, Sandy (a name meaning "defender and protector of humankind"), stands by his side and speaks gracious words, asking me how my family and I are doing lately and when my next talk on evangelization will be at the local Catholic church. Daniel and his mother often ride the bus to get around town because money is scarce. A family friend stands by as well, holding the cake pan. Daniel and Sandy introduce us. I notice immediately that Daniel's mother and their friend are wearing Tau crosses around their necks. Me give a talk on evangelization? It is they who are evangelizing me once again.

In telling the tale I already have hazarded an interpretation, but only a beginning. May I continue my interpretation a little bit longer. To leave off with the story as I have told it so far may be advantageous for givenness. A brief and semi-poetic narrative lends itself to the reader's interpretive imagination. By sharing more of my personal interpretation I risk cluttering up the event with too many details. However, for the sake of demonstrating the necessity of ongoing interpretation in the wake of every self-giving phenomenon, I make a gamble. Perhaps givenness will be added to givenness and not only detracted.

PHENOMENOLOGY

The scene of Daniel's visitation merits much contemplation. I interpret the encounter as a religious event of the highest order. Reminiscent of Mary's visitation of her cousin, Elizabeth, Daniel's visit at the doorstep of my office provokes a response. It ignites an examination of conscience within my soul. In my description above, I try to communicate my personal experience of finitude, that is, limitation. I resist jumping to excuses for my social (let alone charitable) negligence and instead desire an alabaster moment of transparent confession. Why am I so self-interested, self-centered, self-absorbed? What is more attractive about me to myself in comparison with the other who faces me? Is not the other the reason for my own being? Why did I not run out of my office to partake of the celebration for the good of the other? Are the demands on my time so extreme that I am not able to spend some time with Daniel and his family and friends? I am humiliated. I am humiliated on this page as you read it.

A part of me feels that writing is a welcome penitential practice that serves as a form of prayer and as a means to point to heaven. I have confidence that we will have all the time in the world to celebrate in heaven, so maybe my reluctance to join in the party in the here and now comes from the vocation to penance. But, then again, maybe this reluctance comes from the comfort of self-insulation. In any case, I perceive the natural attitude in force within my experience and realize the need for ongoing conversion of it and the looming threat of egocentric centripetal concupiscence that regards the other as an obstacle to the self.

Daniel's visitation was an epiphany—indeed, a theophany. For it was Daniel who saw me, thought of me, and, in a real sense, ran toward me. He reminded me of who I really am and this confirms that the self never could give itself to itself because it depends entirely on the impetus of the other. Outside-of-the-self. He visits me. His blue eyes blaze with truth, sincerity, goodness, hospitality, warmth, hope, yearning. He awaits my response. Will I join in his enterprise of interpersonal communion—that glorious communion extending from eucharistic liturgy? He meets me with the liturgy of dailiness. This ordinary encounter is replete to the point of excess. The uncanny iconic crossing of gazes floods perception with exorbitance. The encounter is saturated with meaning. It is what Caryll Houselander calls an in-breaking of Mount Tabor. It is at once protological and eschatological. Beginning and end. End and beginning. It is judgment day. It is a proleptic anticipation of the judgment that awaits me on the nighttime horizon of my life. I stand not only indicted but invited. The Tau crosses commingle with the dry crumbs of cake and the sweet frosting. Take and eat; this is my body given up for you. A paraliturgical phenomenon that is anchored in the Eucharist itself. A new *missio* in which I am at once summoned and sent. A game of hide-and-go-seek wherein I rejoice because I was found.

Daniel came to me this day as a kind of Christ figure. Not that he merely points to Christ but that he is a genuine vicar of Christ on earth—an *alter Christus*—especially in and through his disabilities in which "power is made perfect in weakness" (2 Cor 12:9). With his visit, hello, and gift of cake, the very gift of salvation is presented in a new key. If you will not come to visit me, I will come to visit you. A metamorphosis of finitude, as Emmanuel Falque puts it. I am elected. I am chosen. "It was not you who chose me, but I who chose you and appointed you to go and bear fruit that will remain, so that whatever you ask the Father in my name he may give you. This I command you: love one another" (John 15:16–17). All this I interpret from Daniel's sudden visit (*exaíphnes*; *Augenblick*; see Mark 13:36; Luke

2:13; Acts 9:3; 1 Cor 15:52) to me, and I could say so much more . . .

My interpretation is tied to my testimony to what I find most essential in the experience. My intentionality met with a counter-intentionality as I encountered a saturation of givenness and meaning. Even if I communicate this event only in semi-poetic fashion, it is because a punctuated narrative of "first, next, then, finally" would not be able to convey the saturation of the experience to the same degree. Giving intuition flooded my intentionality and, even more, the natural attitude that would rather have remained uninterrupted. In the process of interpreting the experience humility is renewed to the measure that I interpret myself as witness to what gives rather than as lord of what I think. Philosophy must let itself be punctured by theology if it is not to devolve into just another dead and lonely exercise of solipsism. The one who believes himself to be more interesting than the interruption of God needs to take himself much less seriously.

IV. INTERPRETATION AND JESUS

The gospels and the tradition of the church present Jesus as someone who welcomed divine interruption—even divine interruption of his own divinity (see Phil 2:5–11). In fact, the divinity revealed in Jesus is one who welcomed the human interruption of divinity. This is one meaning of the incarnation of God the Son. Creation itself is the interruption of eternal divine beatitude. In Jesus is revealed a God who loves to be interrupted and so creates the universe. God has spoken us into being and will speak us into eternity. God has conversed us into existence. Interpersonal relationships live according to the play of conversation. They communicate and so unite a diversity of persons around the givenness of it all. Eternity itself is disclosed as the byproduct of conversation that involves interpretation upon interpretation. All art, music, dance, literature, invention, and technology are interpretive personal responses to what gives. All science worthy of the name is an interpretive personal response to what gives: receptivity to and interpretation of data. Just economics and politics are personal gift in circulation. For the gift to circulate, it must be interpreted as gift.

How does Jesus interpret? The rabbinic tradition of midrash is the key to understanding this how. When Jesus begins his itinerant ministry of healing, teaching, manifesting and proclaiming the kingdom of God, he initiates his public identity as a Jewish rabbi. He is a teacher who calls disciples to himself. Within his rabbinic school are men and women but the inner circle consists of the twelve apostles—those who are called and sent to extend his ministry of healing, teaching and ushering in the kingdom of God. These men are not from the religious or political elite; they are described as ordinary, even as fishermen and tax collectors. Nevertheless Jesus empowers them to become conversant in their common Jewish heritage of midrash. To do so Jesus utilizes the best techniques of the rabbinic tradition: *Peshat, Remez, Derash* and *Sod*. Even if these techniques were codified in the post-temple and post-Talmudic periods (circa AD 70 and following), evidence of them within the teaching of Jesus is on display in the gospels.

PHENOMENOLOGY

The oral tradition of Jewish midrash included various senses of interpreting Torah: the literal meanings (*Peshat*), the allegorical meanings (*Remez*), the comparative meanings (*Derash*), and the mystical meanings (*Sod*). The genius of rabbinic interpretation is its hospitality for a conflict of interpretations. Truth comes to surface through discourse, interpretation, and debate. The living tension between interpretations prevents the collapse of truth to only one of its parts. Rabbinic midrash prevents reductionism. Therefore rabbinic midrash is phenomenological in nature: it prevents the myopia of the natural attitude by extending the task of interpretation, thereby revealing new hidden meanings that escaped first notice. Jesus was a master of midrash, especially because he aimed at the essence of things: the human heart.

If Mary of Nazareth embodies a theology of childhood through her contemplative receptivity to gift, the complementary counterpart is a theology of adulthood: "When I was a child, I used to talk as a child, think as a child, reason as a child; when I became a man, I put aside childish things" (1 Cor 13:11). Contemplation and ethics, love and responsibility, givenness and interpretation. Interpretation fills out what givenness by itself cannot give. In other words, the gift appears to the degree that it is received, or interpreted, as a gift. Jewish midrash, while resisting the idolatry of the sacred, serves as the condition of possibility for receiving givenness in full, that is, beyond measure. Interpretation, though ancillary to givenness, secures the passageway of givenness by describing it and pondering it. Interpretation of givenness through language humanizes perception. We are not merely animals because we rationally interpret the meanings of what we perceive as a collective humanity.

Jesus the rabbi teaches through interpretation. Before sharing a message he stops, looks, and listens. He gathers his media and material for sharing his message by carefully observing the cultural milieu of his audience. Not only does he speak to them, he does life with them. He is one of them, and, because he is one of them, he can teach them effectively, unlocking the plethora of givenness that constitutes the kingdom of God. Jesus's interpretations empower his listeners to interpret in similar ways. He models an intentionality of faith that eclipses the eclipse of the natural attitude in order to throw light on all that gives. The narrative of Jesus's encounter with Zacchaeus, or Zacchaeus's encounter with Jesus (Luke 19:1–10), is a helpful illustration of how Jesus interprets and how he teaches us to interpret.

A. "He came to Jericho and was passing through [*diérchomai*]."

En route to the city of Jerusalem for the final time in his earthly life, Jesus passes through Jericho. Reminiscent of the archetypal encounter of Joshua and the Israelites with the powers of Jericho upon their arrival in Canaan (see Josh 2–6), Jesus's movement through this city signals a new exodus and arrival. The narrative of the encounter between Jesus and Zacchaeus begins with Jesus's intention to visit

Jericho, even if only to pass through it. He does not bypass it but enters it. Jesus is open to encounter and to the possibilities that await him there. The irony is that Jericho, as a historically wealthy and affluent city, was in need of being enriched. Jesus bears a wealth that comes only through voluntary poverty. The book of Joshua recounts the collapse of the walls of Jericho that are symbolic on so many levels. Jesus passes through Jericho in order that the invisible walls of the natural attitude and calloused hearts would come crumbling down.

Jesus passes through Jericho, exposing himself to all the walls he would meet there. So many walls of resistance. The fragrance of Jericho—the name Jericho means "fragrance"—is called by Jesus to give way to "the aroma of Christ" (2 Cor 2:14–15). In his incarnate vulnerability Jesus comes to Jericho to perceive the imperception of those who neither recognized him nor accepted him (see John 1:10–11). However, he leaves open the possibility of conversion, even if the conversion of only one person. Because Jesus intends to pass through the town encounter is made possible. He gives himself over to the possibility of encounter, not just that someone might encounter him but that he might encounter the other as well. Related to the Greek verb *diermeneúo* ("to interpret, explain, translate"), *diérchomai* signifies a coming and going, a crossing over. The prefix *dier*, like the Latin *inter*, means "between." Jesus's passing through Jericho includes an interpretation of it in light of the history of the people of Israel. Jericho lies between where Jesus is and where he needs to go: Jerusalem. He knows he must pass through Jericho but his journey through the town will serve as a microcosm of the salvation revealed in his paschal mystery accomplished in Jerusalem. It is because Jesus elects to pass through (interpret) Jericho that an interpersonal encounter of conversion is made possible.

B. "Now a man there named Zacchaeus ... was seeking to see [*zetéo horáo*] who Jesus was ... So he ran ahead and climbed [*anabaíno*] a sycamore tree in order to see Jesus."

A man named Zacchaeus (meaning "pure and innocent") seeks to see Jesus (meaning "YHWH-saves"). Zacchaeus emulates the paradigmatic intentionality that does justice to givenness. Not only does he seek Jesus, he runs ahead and climbs a sycamore tree in order to see him. The Greek text says that Zacchaeus was short in stature (*helikía mikros*) and that he was unable (*oúk dýnamai*) to see Jesus because of the crowd (*óchlos*). Another translation of *helikía*, other than "height/stature," is "age/maturity." We can interpret not only a lack of physical altitude in Zacchaeus but also perhaps a lack of contemplative and moral maturity. At the same time, the smallness (*mikros*) of Zacchaeus may suggest a contemplative maturity much like the religious potential of the child. Zacchaeus wonders into the territory of encounter and so he wanders in the direction of Jesus. Zacchaeus's ascent (*anabaíno*) of encounter in Jericho anticipates his ascent of encounter at the end of time: his resurrection (*anástasis*). "'What eye has not seen, and ear has not heard, and what has not entered [*anabaíno*] the human heart, what God has prepared for those who love him,' this God has revealed to us through the Spirit" (1 Cor 2:9–10; see Isa 64:3; Luke 24:38). Resurrection is the movement from the impossible/unable (*oúk dýnamai*) to the not impossible/not unable (*oúk adýnamai*; see Luke 1:37). In Zacchaeus's ascent of the sycamore tree is a foretelling of the resurrection, his own and that of Jesus, through the power of the tree of life, the wood of the cross.

PHENOMENOLOGY

Luke's text describes Zacchaeus as a chief tax collector and a wealthy man (*ploúsios*). He was filled with plenty of material goods and social status—the fragrance of Jericho!—but there was something he lacked and so he sought after Jesus. He recognized his natural attitude—including the principle of sufficient reason—to be insufficient for all that possibly could give itself to his perception. In spite of his attempt to encounter Jesus in his epiphany at Jericho, the crowd (*óchlos*) occluded him. What Martin Heidegger calls "the chatter" (*das Gerede*) or what Bernard Lonergan calls "the surd" was preventing the encounter between Zacchaeus and Jesus. Notice that he wanted to notice (*horáo*) Jesus but could not do so until further notice with the help of the stature (*helikía*) of the sycamore tree and the iconic notice (*horáo*) of Jesus. The urgency of Zacchaeus that expresses itself in his running ahead and scaling the fig tree (the tree of life?) shows the importunate importance of bracketing the natural attitude before it is too late and life (Jesus) passes him by.

Interpretation

C. "When he reached the place [*tópos*], Jesus looked up [*anablépo*]."

Here begins the climax of the story. Jesus reaches the place (*tópos*), the place Zacchaeus had run ahead to reach. This is the topography of encounter. An atmosphere and environment ripe for encounter. Zacchaeus becomes undignified in order to encounter his and others' true dignity. The wealthy and honorable, short and childish Zacchaeus up in the tree in order to notice Jesus—in order to have Jesus notice him. Humility is the preamble to majesty. Smallness is the prerequisite of greatness. Humility grants access to the saturating fullness of givenness. Indeed, the humble man gets more than he bargained for. Jesus looks up (*anablépo*) at him, face to face, eye to eye. *Kairós*. This is the today (*sémeron*) of encountering Jesus—today (*sémeron*) as adverb and not today (*heméra*) as noun. This is the verbal time of advent, of ethical relationship and interpersonal communion. It is not the nominative time that can be managed and manipulated like money in the bank or weights on a scale. This is the poetic and creative time of encounter—the time that makes time, time for the other.

Jesus's looking up, *anablépo*, also can be translated "regain one's sight, to be able to see, to restore one's sight" (see John 9:1–41). First, Jesus's look toward Zacchaeus signifies the way God takes a second look at the repentant sinner. When God looks again, God, at the same time, invites the penitent to look again too. This crossing of gazes, exchange of looks, generates an intentionality of faith on the part of the creature evoked by the divine intentionality of mercy. Mercy nurses conversion wherein sight is regained, not only physically but, above all, spiritually. In this case, to see again is to love again. This is the essential meaning even of the healing miracles of Jesus, such as giving sight to the blind.

Not only does Jesus look upon Zacchaeus, he speaks to him: "Zacchaeus, come down quickly [*speúdo katabaíno*], for today [*sémeron*] I must stay [*méno*] at your house [*oikía*]." First, Jesus addresses Zacchaeus by name, in effect speaking innocence and purity back into him. He tells him to come down quickly (*speúdo*), as is fitting for the one "waiting [*prosdokáo*] and hastening [*speúdo*] the coming [*parousía*] of the day of God" (2 Pet 3:12). And Zacchaeus is obedient. He comes down from the tree quickly (*speúdo*), just as Mary "set out and traveled to the hill country in haste [*spoudé*]" (Luke 1:39) to visit Elizabeth. The descent (*katábasis*) of Zacchaeus mirrors his paradoxical ascent (*anabaíno*) of humility. It alludes to the *katábasis* of proud peoples and nations (see Isa 14:13–15; Luke 10:13–16). The natural attitude of self-inflation and self-insulation must descend from its lofty heights of isolation and alienation. Zacchaeus must dismount from his molehill to reach the mountain of Christ, precisely back into the thick of the crowd to witness to the possibility of conversion and the goodness of sociality. Upon Mary's encounter with Elizabeth in her home, the infant (John the Baptist) in Elizabeth's womb "leaped for joy [*skirtáo*]" (Luke 1:44). In a similar way, upon his encounter with Jesus, Zacchaeus descended the sycamore tree "and received [*hypodéchomai*]" Jesus "with joy [*chará*]." Zacchaeus exemplifies the response of authenticity before the givenness of the gift (*cháris*): joy. Joy is the sure sign that the kingdom of God has come near (see Matt 13:44; Luke 1:14; 2:10). Zacchaeus's receptivity (*hypodéchomai*) to Jesus entails receiving the other as a guest. Again, this intentionality of hospitality is instructive for pedagogy in phenomenology: every phenomenon is to be received as a guest. An intentionality of receptivity, in turn, propagates not only contemplation but also social responsibility in the form of hospitality.

Jesus offers Zacchaeus the proleptic eucharistic gift of himself by way of inviting himself over. Jesus invites and empowers Zacchaeus to the gesture of hospitality that is certain evidence of his conversion. Jesus's visitation to the home of Zacchaeus involves further humiliation as it is followed by ridicule of some in the crowd who remain (*méno*) in the grumbling natural attitude: "When they all saw this, they began to grumble [*goggýzo*], saying, 'He has gone to stay at the house of a sinner.'" Many in the crowd chatter on and reinforce the surd of the natural attitude. What exquisite paradox: "I came into the world for judgment, so that those who do not see might see, and those who do see might become blind . . . If you were blind, you would have no sin; but now you are saying, 'We see,' so your sin remains" (John 9:39, 41; see 1 John 1:8). Either one acknowledges the deficiencies of the natural attitude, admits his sinful status, and invites Jesus to abide (*méno*) with him and so sees, or one abides (*méno*) in the natural attitude, denies the invitation to conversion, rejects the givenness of the gospel of Jesus, and so remains (*méno*) blind. One either can tradition (*paradídomi*) the gospel or betray (*paradídomi*) it.

If, for Martin Heidegger, language is the house of being, the story of Zacchaeus reveals that hospitality is the house (*oikía*) of givenness. So much hospitality, so much givenness. The encounter of interpersonal givenness between Jesus and Zacchaeus continues all the way to Zacchaeus's home. Beyond the contemplative encounter of saturating givenness, an ethical upshot transcends the immanence of what gives. Through language and interpretation an intersubjective relationship is established that issues its own exigencies outside of the immanent data of embodied perception and consciousness. As Emmanuel Levinas contends, the face of the other is not a datum of givenness, not an appearance among appearances or just another phenomenon manifest. Rather, the face of the other is ethical signification, call and even accusation. I am its witness and my responsibility for the other is its evidence.

Zacchaeus assumes responsibility to host Jesus, but not only that. He also accepts responsibility for his fraudulent and irresponsible history in relation to all persons toward which he has acted negligently: "Behold, half of my possessions, Lord, I shall give [*dídomi*] to the poor, and if I have extorted anything from anyone I shall repay [*apodídomi*] it four times over." Responsibility becomes incarnate as money, food, possessions, and embodied service toward the naked face of the other. The givenness that met Zacchaeus in his encounter with Jesus spurs on Zacchaeus to become givenness through his ethical status as agent responsible. He is enabled and inspired by Jesus to become responsible before the face of the other. This is the meaning of Eucharist as circulation of ethical gift. The lifeblood of this ethical gift circulates to and from the pulsating heart of the home, even (and especially) when one is homeless.

D. "Today [*sémeron*] salvation [*sotería*] has come to this house because this man too is a descendent of Abraham. For the Son of Man has come to seek [*zetéo*] and to save [*sózo*] what was lost [*apóllymi*]."

"'In an acceptable time [*kairós*] I heard you, and on the day of salvation I helped you.' Behold, now [*nyn*] is a very acceptable time [*kairós*]; behold, now [*nyn*] is the day of salvation" (2 Cor 6:2). The today/now (*sémeron/nyn*) of the time (*kairós*) of encounter continues with Zacchaeus's welcome of Jesus into his home. Jesus identifies Zacchaeus as a son of Abraham inasmuch as he has received him according to his

Interpretation

intentionality of faith. Contemplation and responsibility for the other are the essence of salvation. This is the fig of the tree. The sweetness and fruitfulness are here. Salvation and God are not something on the side of the other but come precisely within the face-to-face encounter, within ethical exigency, within righteous responsibility. Zacchaeus's encounter with Jesus, including the welcoming of him into his home and his conversion to justice and mercy, was a foretaste of heaven—that eternal rendezvous of welcome. Just as Zacchaeus sought Jesus as he made his way into Jericho, Jesus reveals the mission of the Son of Man (the mission of Jesus): "to seek and to save what was lost" (Luke 19:10). Another way to say this is to cure what was dead and ruined. This is the merciful power of God revealed in Christ: not only to create from nothing (*ex nihilo*) but to redeem from less than nothing.

Interpretation supplies the time (*kairós*) of redemption. This time has no limits except for the final countdown of judgment that only serves to prolong this *kairós* of merciful eternity. Judgment, too, merits an inexhaustible interpretation that lifts the veil of the boundless train of givenness to peer modestly and chastely beneath its saturating deluge of meanings. Jesus teaches us how to interpret by inviting us to interpret. He seems to be less about providing us with definitive interpretations, although on occasion he does so, and more about provoking questions that cause us to interpret the givenness manifest and responsibility proclaimed oftentimes implicitly and enigmatically: "Who do people say that the Son of Man is? . . . But who do you say that I am?" (Matt 16:13b, 15).

V. DIALECTICAL INTERPRETATION

Albert Einstein purportedly said, "The important thing is not to stop questioning." This statement gets at the heart of the meaning of interpretation. Interpretation is led by its questions. Once we no longer have any questions, we no longer have anything to interpret. This is something tragic that can happen (even often) in education: your students show up to class with no questions. When this happens, as a professor, I feel that if my students have no questions to ask, then I have nothing to teach. Further, as a professor, if I have run out of questions to ask, then I have nothing to explore and, therefore, nothing to teach. Scientific investigation depends entirely on its questions, and this is true for theology as well. Theology: the science of God. Theology deals at all times with questions about God, and the material for theological experiments includes all the data of life, logical deliberation and divine revelation. The above scene of encounter between Zacchaeus and Jesus is an episode of divine revelation for Christian theology. Not only is it understood as divine revelation because it is an excerpt of the canonical biblical text, but also because of the nature of its contents: a narrative relating an interpersonal encounter between Zacchaeus and Jesus. The details of this story have a lot to say about the pattern of encounter with God as revealed in Jesus.

Judeo-Christian interpretation is dialectical in character. This means that interpretation happens around the good complementary polarity of ideas and, above all, around the diversity of interlocutors or persons involved in the conversation. If there is one thing that authentic Judaism and Christianity are not, it is fundamentalism. Fundamentalism implies reductionism. Fundamentalism is another name for the natural attitude, whether it takes the form of religious fundamentalism, scientific fundamentalism, ideological fundamentalism, or any other brand of fundamentalism. Fundamentalism reduces the whole to only one or some of its many parts. Moreover, it confuses the whole for one or some of its parts. A common reductionism of the twenty-first century is material reductionism. Stemming from the dialectical materialism of Karl Marx, Friedrich Engels, Joseph Stalin and others, and coupled with an atheistic (or at least agnostic) ideology reinforced by (at least a caricature of) Darwinian evolutionary theory, a worldview infused with material reductionism is sweeping the globe like wildfire. For instance, in the United States STEM education is trending like never before. Secondary school curricula are being reduced to the disciplines of (natural) science, technology, engineering and mathematics, as if these are the only fields of study adolescents need to be successful and thrive in the world today. It is almost to suggest that we would be better off living as robots and machines rather than as human beings. What about the humanities, music, the arts, literature, philosophy, and theology? Since the origin of the university, theology was regarded as "the queen of all sciences" because of the questions it asks and the material of its investigation. Instead of being taught how to think, young people are being taught what to think. This is what Pope Francis has called "ideological colonization."

PHENOMENOLOGY

However, the good news is that the art of holistic interpretation will continue to unmask the unwarranted reductionisms that crop up in culture, even if our haunting histories of fundamentalist wars (including today's terrorist movements of whatever stripe), genocide, and ecological degradation fail to haunt us. Interpretation is the gateway to givenness. It is the voice that goes before and behind every phenomenon, saying, "Wait, there's more." There is more to interpret. There is more to investigate. There is more to witness. There is more to give. There are more ways to be responsible for the other who faces me. The whole is greater than its parts, and even greater than the sum of its parts. Dialectical interpretation is the midrashic method of the rabbis, the method of Jesus. Truth comes to surface through the play of conversation as led by the question. Unity requires diversity. For there to be genuine unity, diverse parts are brought together. Otherwise, there is only more of the same. Dialectical interpretation recognizes the givenness of order: united diversity, diverse unity. It refuses reductionism and renounces every fundamentalism that masquerades as the fullness of truth when it runs with only one of its parts and, therefore, disintegrates the meaning of the part in relation to the whole from which it was taken.

Jesus teaches his listeners not to close the door on possibility. He teaches us to listen more attentively, to welcome more warmly, to love more yearningly. Personal encounter with Jesus, not only by way of theological imagination and memory but also by way of living prayer, sacramental intimacy, and ethical responsibility for the other, opens the labyrinth of interpretation as enveloped in a womb of givenness. "For at the moment the sound of your greeting reached my ears, the infant in my womb [*koilía*] leaped for joy" (Luke 1:44). World is womb. Are we studious in relation to this womb? Do questions well up in us that lead us to the threshold of divine revelation and its possibility? Or have we become accustomed to putting borders around the questions we permit ourselves to ask? Yes, philosophy and reason lead us to this theological threshold of inquiry so much so that the best methods in philosophy have vast potential to be put to work inside of theological questions. Encounter with Jesus invites this possibility of interpreting all the way to the crossing of the limit because the limen between the possible and the impossible simply marks the passover to a surplus of possibility. And this statement, too, invites interpretation.

Key chapter concepts: interpretation, hermeneutics, intentionality, fundamentalism, reductionism, saturated phenomenon, midrash, Torah, Talmud, dialectic

DISCUSSION QUESTIONS

1. What does interpretation have to do with givenness and how can interpretation obstruct givenness?

PHENOMENOLOGY

2. Metaphysics explains and phenomenology describes. What is the difference between explaining and describing and how do these two distinct tasks complement one another?

3. Have you ever had an experience like the one the author describes in his encounter with Daniel? Talk about your experience and how you were surprised and changed by the revelation of the other.

4. How does the story of Zacchaeus teach us about the art of phenomenological interpretation?

5. What is meant by "dialectical interpretation" and how do we prevent a collapse of the dialectic?

4

PARADOX

IN THE PREVIOUS THREE chapters phenomenology has been shown to be a method committed to possibility. It is a method of thought or even a way of life—a lifestyle that defends the possible and allows for hope in it. Chapter 3 ended with a reflection on dialectical interpretation that is faithful to possibility and to all that may give itself by itself. Interpretation in phenomenology describes not only what gives but also those patterns of givenness that make up the paradigmatic self-revelation of truth. It is not that phenomenology is unconcerned with questions of truth. Phenomenology is adamant about deciphering with accuracy and precision what gives itself. It is obsessed with drawing distinctions between what is authentic and what is inauthentic in relation to questions in morality and ethics. For phenomenology, givenness is truth and so are the patterns of what gives and how it gives. Truth gives itself by itself. I do not determine it as if I were the creator of the universe. Truth reveals itself through coherent structures of meaning or patterns of givenness.

One integral pattern observed quickly in phenomenology is paradox. The term *paradox* signifies possibility—in fact, the possibility of possibility. Paradox means a unity of plurality, both/and, yes and yes. Paradox describes the very structure of all phenomenality—a unity of diverse elements that constitute every personal experience: the phenomenon, the self, and the interaction between the two. Phenomenality, or the realm of experience, is formed by a communion of parts. Every experience forms a unity but only in and through its diversity of parts. Is experience one? Yes. Is experience manifold, polyvalent, heterogeneous? Yes. Both/and. Paradox denotes the phenomenality of all experience because paradox expresses possibility as the impossibility of impossibility. Is anything impossible? Yes: impossibility. This is a paradox. Paradox holds eternal possibility as its primary point of reference. Paradox allows givenness to keep on giving. It does not call foul when there is no foul. It does not pronounce death when there is no death. It does not close the door on love, forgiveness, and resurrection from the dead when these remain the most impossibly impossible possibilities for human experience. Paradox is the chief phenomenon because it describes the essential character of all phenomenality, ruled as it is by possibility.

I. PARADOX

Derived from the Greek word *parádoxos* ("incredible, unusual, unexpected, uncommon, wonderful"), the English word *paradox* hovers above the borderlands of contradiction and the transgression of the impossible. From its Greek roots, *para* ("beside, beyond") *dóxa* ("opinion, glory"), the

Paradox

meaning of paradox means more than one thing at once. It can mean two opinions or beliefs side by side, that is, two points of view held together in tension all the while wanting some resolution in one direction or the other but never having simple resolution. An example of this phenomenon taken from the world of natural science is light. Is light a wave or a particle? Both. It depends on how it is measured and observed. Again, from a global perspective, is it day or night? Both. It depends on what side of the globe you are at a given point in time. Always in reference to the either/or metaphysical principle of noncontradiction, paradox insists on another principle in force at the same time: the principle of possibility. Whereas the principle of noncontradiction claims (and rightly so) that a thing cannot be what it is and not be what it is at the same time ($A=A$, $A \neq -A$)—also closely related to the principle of identity and difference, which claims that a thing is what it is and not what it is not ($A=A$, $A \neq B$)—the principle of possibility considers the possibility of phenomena that adhere to the rational principles of metaphysics and yet go beyond them. This is the other meaning of paradox: the beyond of glory that saturates pedestrian and mundane being.

The term *paradox*, as used in phenomenology, does not mean an unsolvable riddle but a phenomenon that gives an abundance of meaning precisely because it means more than one thing at once. A paradox generates meaning by virtue of its saturating phenomenality. Another example of paradox is the literary play of metaphor, allegory, symbolism, and analogy. These types of literary devices help create more meanings than pedantic correspondences of sign–referent or concept–percept. For example, the metaphor "your love is a song" generates meaning that two side-by-side dictionary definitions of love and song otherwise would not mean. The metaphor is productive of meaning through the phenomenon of paradox. Its play of meaning is based on the is/is not distinction within the assertion: (1) your love is a song, and (2) your love is not a song. To say "your love is a song" means many things in spite of the metaphysical fact that love is not a song per se. "Your love is a song" could mean that your love is beautiful, sonorous, harmonious, pleasing, delightful, praiseworthy, ordered, metered, flowing, moving, emotional, musical, collaborative, meaningful, creative, fun, stirring, expressive, communicable, etc. Because of the is/is not distinction of the metaphor, the paradox exploits the principle of noncontradiction by making it profitable and productive of meaning that transgresses the facile reductionism of the either/or. Love is not a song and a song is not love. However, thanks to the logic of paradox, I can say in truth that love is a song.

Applied to the concept of God, paradox brings life and creativity to the theological imagination that by necessity is always an analogical imagination. Does God exist? Yes and no. The concept of God gives itself. However, God, by definition, is that which exceeds all concepts, even that of God. To speak of God's existence defies all categories of being, even that of existence. Although we can approximate knowledge of God by way of analogy, we never can "pin the tail on God" adequately or exhaustively with our host of concepts unworthy of divinity. In the end, to know God is to be known by God (see 1 Cor 8:1–3; Gal 4:9), and this is a paradox indeed. For every theism there must be a concomitant atheism in order to prevent the saturating meaning of God to slip into another fundamentalist caricature. Idolatry signifies this collapse of God into some manageable household deity that is treated more like a genie in a bottle than almighty divinity that is able to bring good even out of evil, above all through incarnation and resurrection.

Paradox

Phenomenology prevents the static fundamentalisms of metaphysics and its legion of onto-theologies. Phenomenology prohibits the limitation of divinity to the insufficient categories of being and causality. However, as a double-edged sword phenomenology must be subject to critique in order to avert its own fundamentalisms in the forms of phenomenalism, relativism, skepticism, and nihilism. In the end, metaphysics is necessary to counteract the tendency of phenomenology's greatest strength to become its greatest weakness. Possibility must be reintroduced to actuality and the categories of being in order to deflect the promiscuous idolatry of possibility masquerading as an undiscerning connoisseur of everything under the sun. This is the haunting distinction between realism and idealism that must be faced time and time again. The relationship between phenomenology and metaphysics is the great methodological paradox that promotes the fullness of givenness, truth and being to come to fruition. This is the place where paradoxy (as any opinion) and orthodoxy (as right belief) meet. Judgment can be suspended only for so long, but then one must risk a definitive decision of belief. Warrant for such a decision comes ultimately from the immovable epistemological anchor of metaphysics.

II. PARADOX AND EMPATHY

As human beings, paradox is incredibly helpful for understanding the possibility of empathy within interpersonal relationships. Since the meaning of empathy (*em-páscho*) is to bear the experience/suffering of the other within the self, the logic of paradox secures the rights of this possibility and describes its phenomenal manifestation and ethical signification. In the phenomenon of empathy the experience of the other is impregnated within the self. Empathy refers to a visceral, embodied, spiritual and deeply personal phenomenon. It entails the meaning of compassion and meaningful suffering: to bear up the other in her suffering and to endure the dramatic trial together. Empathy involves solicitude for the other. From its Greek and Latin roots, *holos/sollus* ("whole") *ciere* ("to move"), solicitude refers to a movement of the entire self, body and soul, at the sway of the other and her experience. When I empathize I am moved to deep anxiety and concern over the plight of the other. I become preoccupied by the suffering and death of the other even more than my own suffering and death. Empathy is the gateway to the life of heroic virtue since it makes possible self-forgetfulness before the remembrance (anamnesis) of the other. The hero is the one who puts the life and needs of the other before his own and therefore lives in radical responsibility toward the other who faces him.

It is a paradox that the experience of the other would transfer—at least to some degree—within the experience of the self. For the experience of the other is one thing and my experience is another. But for the experience of the other to take its place in me implies a veritable unity of diverse experiences—these respective spiritual phenomena that commingle as one. Perhaps this is an indication of the potential unity of angels, saints, and divinity in their fiercely gentle, chaste, modest, and responsible intimate interpersonal communion of love. Borrowing the theological concept of Trinitarian *perichóresis/circumincessio*—the mutual indwelling and interpersonal circulation of the three Persons of the Trinity—empathy intuits and anticipates the potential of the I and the you to form a we. This is the anthropological essence of solidarity between persons. The paradoxical phenomenon of empathy dilates the soul to make room for the other, beginning with prayerful and contemplative solicitude for the good of the other.

Empathy showcases the power of paradox because it signifies not only a logic of paradox but one involving the inter-punctuation of persons. It expresses the paradox of transcendence and immanence commingling in a diversified unity. The radical transcendent otherness of the other—the other who is precisely not identical to me—is shared through the intimately immanent manifestation of the other within the same. In empathy the otherness of the other sustains its irreducible otherness all the while sharing this incommunicable otherness within the heart of the self. Through empathy I am able to receive the other not only as idea, phenomenon, friend or foe, but as s/he gives her/himself to me in her/his transcendent glory of otherness yet through her/his immanent advent of vulnerable infancy within myself. In empathy the experience of the other gestates within me as a child grows and develops within her mother's womb. As a cardinal paradox within human experience, empathy helps us understand not only the logic of paradox but also its saturating beauty. Let us transition now to consider the paradoxical relationship between freedom and responsibility, held together by the phenomenon of empathy, in everyday life.

III. PARADOX IN EVERYDAY LIFE

Up to this point in the book we have witnessed the ability of phenomenology to unlock the power of possibility for human experience. At the same time we have observed that by possibility is not meant anything goes. A great paradox about possibility is that the unlimited is revealed in and through the limited. On one hand, phenomenology has the potential to describe with precision any and all phenomena, whatever they may be, all the while suspending a final verdict on the moral goodness or ontological truth of the phenomena. On the other hand, astute phenomenology cannot help deciphering between that which affords an increase in genuine possibility and that which subtracts from possibility. Responsible phenomenology calls a thing what it is and does not capitulate according to any form of ideology or fundamentalism. Responsible phenomenology is neither

Paradox

liberal nor conservative, neither Democrat nor Republican, neither left-wing nor right-wing. In truth phenomenology is neither/nor because it is not either/or. It is both/and. It is all of the above. It is yes and yes and yes. Phenomenology operates according to the logic of paradox because it is this logic that gives itself before and behind every phenomenal appearance and ethical signification. May the following narrative help illuminate the meaning of paradoxical truth, dialectical interpretation, and obedient hermeneutics.

Born on February 24, 1978, in Kalamazoo, Michigan, I was given up for adoption the same day. After living with a foster family for six weeks I was adopted by John and Linda Wallenfang of Benton Harbor, Michigan. Upon being adopted, my adoptive father and mother gave me a name: Donald Lee Wallenfang, taken from the names of my grandfathers, Donald Shultz and Lee Wallenfang. I was given a name that was not my own by a family that was not my own, but they became my own through adoption. And so the paradox begins. Two distinct identities joined as one through the act of adoption. I am initiated as a Wallenfang for life and my adoptive parents are initiated as parents of me for life. The phenomenon of family itself is paradoxical. Is it one? Yes. Is it many? Yes. A unity of a plurality of persons that together form a communion of persons in love and responsibility for one another. This is at once the power and possibility of family life. Its permanence, its fidelity, its diverse unity, its united diversity, its integrity, its wholeness, its solidarity, its solicitude, its empathy, its nuclear composition in relation to other families and the whole of society, its freedom.

Did John and Linda Wallenfang become more free when they adopted me? Did I become more free when they adopted me? Some might argue that John and Linda became less free when they adopted me because they assumed more responsibility in life: to care for me and to raise me for many years to come. This argument would be based on an either/or alternative between freedom and responsibility, as if these are mutually exclusive concepts. More responsibility equals less freedom and more freedom equals less responsibility. At first glance this logic seems to stand to reason. The more responsibilities I have for other people in my life, the less I am able to move about freely and do what I want with no accountability to anyone else. The fewer responsibilities I have for people in my life, the more I can be preoccupied with my own needs, desires, and wants. For this hermeneutic of freedom and responsibility the primary point of reference is the ego, the self. It lacks imagination because it lacks the powerful possibility of paradox. Instead of confining itself to an either/or imagination, the logic of paradox is on the lookout for the fruitfulness and fecundity of the both/and. Is there a freedom that might be opened up precisely in and through the privilege of responsibility for the other who faces me? Yes, and it goes by the name of love.

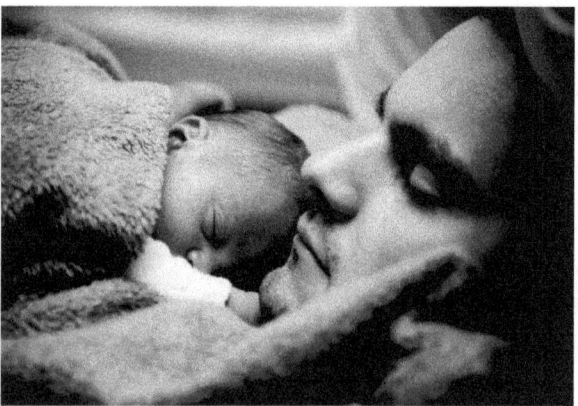

According to the paradoxical freedom of love, John and Linda entered into an even more expansive freedom when they adopted me: the freedom of the gift. This is a

Paradox

freedom sequestered and accessed only through obedient responsibility for the other. They could not have experienced the freedom of fatherhood and motherhood without being initiated into it by my permanent visitation. The proximity of persons in vulnerable responsibility for one another is the condition of possibility for the freedom of love. Interpreting the other person, in the nakedness of his or her face, as call, as gift, as precious, as treasure, as sacred, and as witness to the infinite ruptures like an earthquake the selfishness of the self and sets the ego free from itself. There is a blind spot of bondage that goes unrecognized most often: the bondage of the self to itself. As if the self exists for its own sake alone! As if that is the heroic meaning of life! Being toward death—as if my own death is my chief concern amidst the plethora of possibilities of self-donation, one-for-the-other! In fact, this self-concern is inimical to freedom and the sociality of freedom because it interprets the freedom of the other in competition with my own. It interprets the whole of the social order as a zero-sum game, a win-lose dichotomy. Rather there remains the possibility of a coexistence of freedoms that is promoted to the degree of responsibility we exercise in relation to one another, for one another. The vocation to live as my brother's and sister's keeper marks the universal human vocation absolutely.

It is this responsible freedom—the freedom of the gift that is impregnated with the heights of possibility—that John and Linda Wallenfang entered into six weeks after my birth. It was the freedom lived by my biological mother (at least), who chose to bring me to birth and give me up for adoption. In a post-*Roe v. Wade* (1973) United States, she could have "terminated her pregnancy" (namely, me) without legal repercussions, without a sign or trace of me any longer in her body, but forever in her memory, even as a remote what if. Instead, she chose the yes of life-giving possibility in the middle of her impossibility. It was her refusal of this impossibility that led to greater possibility, just as it was the refusal of their experience of infertility that led John and Linda to adopt me. Interpreting the other who faces me as gift—even if his face is deformed, lined with wrinkles, or still developing in the womb—expands the territory of freedom to encompass the freedom of every person. At the margins of the gift is still gift.

As to the second question raised above, did I become more free when John and Linda adopted me. Without question, yes. Responsibility reveals itself as the necessary condition of possibility for freedom, beginning with the freedom to live. The human species is one of the most altricial species within the animal kingdom. Human offspring remain immature and in need of parental care and nourishment longer than any other species of comparable size. Parental responsibility is a prerequisite for ensuring the freedom of the child. Our altricial nature attests to our vulnerability and radical interdependence on one another as well as on a healthy biosphere in which to thrive. Through paternal and maternal empathy the child's holistic formation is secured. Empathetic responsibility for the other describes the basic anthropological vocation with great precision. To live for the other and to let her life share itself within my own, altogether forming an interpersonal we of solidarity, expands the range of possibilities within the human experience, especially the possibilities of love. For love is tried and tested within the kiln of suffering when the struggle of the other who faces me becomes my own.

Adoption exemplifies the paradoxical relationship between freedom and responsibility, between liberty and empathy. The self is set free joyously from itself when it responds *fiat* before the call of the other. A great escape—indeed ecstasy—is made when the ego forgets itself in the

Paradox

affective wave of solicitude for the other. In effect, I save my life when I lose it, but not only is my own life saved (see Matt 10:39). As I lose my life—spending my time, my energy, my money, my thoughts, my rights, my body, my soul—for the sake of the other (even all the way to substitution!) the other lives all the more ... and so do I. When I lose myself in self-forgetfulness I become my true self in other-remembrance that takes the form of self-abnegating service. Through a brief phenomenological analysis the highest possibilities of the ego reveal themselves when the ego is oriented not around itself but around the other facing me. The ego moves when it faces the other and goes toward the other. Otherwise the ego clings to itself in its static misery of empty arrogance, arrogating to itself what is not its own.

The great paradox of the call of the other is that it is seldom heard from the mouth of the other. Instead it wells up in me as an ethical exigence, a voice of conscience, a movement of spirit, a sensibility of vocation. It is a paradox that the highest possibility for human activity is led by the passive agency of the *fiat mihi*—let it be done unto me. Responsibility for the other begins and is sustained by the unwavering yes to the call of the other. This is where self-care and self-donation merge together as one authentic movement of the human. Adoption demonstrates the heights of this possibility in which the infant—literally, the one without a voice—speaks audibly through the voices of the mother and father who call her by name. Her personal call and givenness are attested prophetically in the voices of her witnesses. It is this prophetic witness to responsibility that is manifest and proclaimed in the life of Jesus of Nazareth, toward which we now will turn.

IV. PARADOX AND JESUS

As is commonly known, Jesus taught primarily through parables. This was a teaching technique already in use within the Jewish community, but Jesus intensifies its affluence through amplified hyperbole, contrast and paradox. Related to the words *paradox* and *parabola*, a parable (*para-* "beside, beyond"; *bállo* "to throw, offer, give") is a narrative that throws two worlds of meaning together in dialectical confrontation. For Jesus's teaching, the throwing together of these two worlds of meaning is for the purpose of provoking belief (*dóxa*) and trust in YHWH and, more specifically, in Jesus, as YHWH's definitive self-revelation, and his message and gift. For instance, when Jesus taught about the kingdom of God, he frequently used parables. One example is the parable of the lost coin (see Luke 15:8–10). Every detail of the parable is pregnant with meaning since each detail serves as a sign pointing to the givenness of the kingdom of God. A woman. Ten coins. One lost coin. Lighting a lamp. Sweeping the house. Searching carefully until she finds it. Calling together friends and neighbors to share her joy over finding it. Jesus concludes the parable by saying, "In just the same way, I tell you, there will be rejoicing among the angels of God over one sinner who repents."

This parable of the woman and the lost coin brings together (1) the common human experience of losing something and finding it and (2) the mystery of the kingdom of God. Jesus uses images that are quite familiar and immanent to describe something that is rather remote and transcendent. A brief uncritical exegesis of the parable, thinking phenomenologically, might go something like this. The woman represents all of humanity, as well as divinity, especially through her feminine genius of receptivity to gift and maternal empathy. She exhibits great solicitude for the lost coin and yearns to find it and gather it back together with the rest. Ten coins symbolize completeness and one of their number missing suggests incompleteness and unevenness. All of the coins represent humanity and the lost coin signifies a human being who has become lost in sin and forgetful of God. The lit lamp refers to the light of Christ, the light of the gospel, and the light of the church. It is the light that illuminates the darkness and allows the lost coin to be found. Sweeping the house calls to mind asceticism, purification, and determined determination (Teresa of Jesus) to find the lost coin. It gives to imagination an image of the hard work and perseverance needed by the missionary church to carry on the mission of Christ: "to seek and to save what was lost" (Luke 19:10). Further, the detail of searching carefully suggests great solicitude at the heart of this soteriological mission to invite fellow sinners to conversion. Finally, the communal joy upon finding the lost coin expresses the eschatological rendezvous of redemption composed of the communion of angels and saints in the company of the Trinity. Jesus's tag line to the parable makes it clear that the lost coin is meant to be interpreted as a sinner who repents and comes home to the Lord through the church. On the whole the parable conveys the eloquent paradox of mundane experience and the revelation of the kingdom of God. Every human experience in some way discloses and conceals this mystery.

In order to ponder the paradoxical nature of Jesus's parables and ministry, let us consider three more key images from the gospels in brief: (1) Jesus's healing of a paralytic man, (2) the concept of exceedance or abundance (*perisseúo*), and (3) the meaning of a man and woman becoming one flesh in the sacrament of marriage.

PHENOMENOLOGY

A. "Then astonishment [*ékstasis*] seized them all and they glorified [*doxázo*] God, and, struck with awe [*pímplemi phóbos*], they said, 'We have seen incredible things [*parádoxa*] today [*sémeron*].'"

The story of Jesus's miraculous healing of a paralyzed man (Luke 5:17–26) is apropos for our understanding of the phenomenality of paradox. Like his parables, Jesus's healing miracles are laced with paradox, specifically in how they transgress the alleged limits of the natural order (*para-* "beyond"; *dóxa* "opinion/glory"). The glory of God radiates through these merciful healings that in turn serve as signs pointing beyond the wonder of temporal psychosomatic reintegration. These miracles or signs bear an anagogical meaning that says something about the life to come, the heavenly life. They are paradigmatic signs of resurrection—a foretaste of the transfigured life to come as an eschatological reintegration of redeemed human persons enfolded in the holistic movement of cosmic redemption (see Rom 8:18–25; 2 Pet 3:12–13; Rev 21:1). This is the highest possibility for all that gives: that it would keep on giving into eternity.

In Luke's text recounting Jesus's healing of the paralyzed man, several revelatory details are worth observing. First, the account witnesses that "the power of the Lord [*dýnamis kyríou*] was with him for healing [*iáomai*]." This is the same power (*dýnamis*) that makes all things possible (*dynatós*; see Luke 18:27). The man to be restored is described as paralyzed (*paralelyménos*). From the Greek root *paralýo*, "to loosen, disable, paralyze," Jesus brings a solution (*lýsis*) to a problem that poses as beyond solution (*pará-lyse*). As deliverer (*lytrotés*) Jesus will unloosen (*lytróomai*) and release/forgive (*apolýo*) that which was lost (*apólese*), much like the lost coin mentioned above (see

Luke 15:9). He will unloosen/resolve (*lýne*) what was loosened (*paralýo*). He will empower (*dýnamai*) what was disempowered (*adýnamai*). The separation/divorce/enmity (*lýsis*) between God and humanity, brought about by humanity's sinfulness, Jesus has come to separate (*apolýo*) by the solution (*lýsis*) of his eucharistic self-gift. Jesus has come to betray (*paradídomi*) the betrayal (*parádosis*) through the traditioning (*paradídomi*) of love and its tradition (*parádosis*). This is the logic of the double negative. To unloosen that which was loosed by becoming bound. To disable disability by becoming disabled. To save that which was lost by losing loss and experiencing God-forsakenness. To abandon abandonment by becoming abandoned—by loving to the point of absolute abandonment. All this Jesus does through his own suffering, death, and resurrection. This is the logic of paradox, the logic of the cross, the logic of divine love.

When Jesus first sees the paralyzed man being lowered on a stretcher through the roof, Jesus says to him, "Man [*ánthrope*], your sins are forgiven [*aphíemi*]." In other words, the debt is canceled, the divorce is divorced, the separation is separated, the forsaken is forsaken, the left behind is left behind, the loss is lost. Jesus declares repair, restoration, and healing for the man—for humankind. Further, Jesus says to the man, "Rise [*egeíro*] and walk." The verb "to raise" used here also can mean to raise from the dead. Jesus has come to deliver much more than allowing the paralyzed man to walk for a time and then eventually die. Jesus has come to offer eternal life that is signaled especially by his proclamation of forgiveness of sins and implicit resurrection from the dead. And what is the healed man's response to all of this? He went home (*oikía*) as Jesus commanded him, "glorifying [*doxázo*] God." The destination of encounter with Jesus is home—a new home, a transfigured home, a redeemed home. Just like Zacchaeus, the unnamed healed man (me?) is sent home to glorify God. This new doxology is one with the perichoretic doxology resounding eternally from the heart of the Trinity. The man glorifies (*doxázo*) God because he has witnessed a paradox (*parádoxa*) in his very flesh and soul of unprecedented proportion.

And the response of the crowd to all of this? "Then astonishment [*ékstasis*] seized them all and they glorified [*doxázo*] God, and, struck with awe [*pímplemi phóbos*], they said, 'We have seen incredible things [*parádoxa*] today [*sémeron*].'" As a result of the adverbial day (*sémeron*) of salvation breaking into the present (*parousía*), the people are seized with ecstasy (*ékstasis*) due to the saturating meaning and power of the event. The friends of the paralyzed man had brought him to Jesus, hoping to "set him in his presence [*enópion*]" (Luke 5:18b). For the presence/notice (*enópion*) of Jesus is the creative and dynamic time of the present (*parousía*). Notice the connection between this reference to the presence/notice of Jesus and Jesus's teaching about the notice (*enópion*) of God in Luke 12 (see chapter 2 of this book). Because Jesus notices the paralyzed man, his sins are forgiven, his locomotion is restored, his

Paradox

joy is reignited, and the eschaton is revealed in the event. The people are filled/finished with fear/awe (*pímplemi phóbos*)—they literally are soaked (*pímplemi*) in fear/awe just as the sponge on a reed was soaked (*pímplemi*) with wine to give drink to Jesus at the limen of his death on the cross (see Matt 27:48). The people attest that they have witnessed incredible things (*parádoxa*)—a saturation of givenness, a host of saturated phenomena. The paradox of their experience of fear reflects the paradox of the entire event: a paralyzed man walks, a sorrowful and desperate man glorifies God, a carpenter teaches and heals, a man forgives sins, disability is disabled through disability, God is revealed in the flesh as incarnate Word, the one who notices God is noticed by God, the people are seized with fear only to the point of this fear being transfigured into wonder and awe. A saturation of saturation transpires in which divine majesty is manifest precisely in and through humility, meekness, empathy, and limitation. Divine love would have it no other way. Finitude is the infinite's chosen means of manifestation. Humility is the glory of divinity's elected pathway of proclamation. Paradox of paradoxes: "you will see greater [*meízon*] things than this" (John 1:50; see John 14:12; 1 John 3:2). And for divine love this greatness always will take the form of humility, servanthood, and self-donation: "Let the greatest among you be as the youngest, and the leader as the servant. For who is greater: the one seated at table or the one who serves? Is it not the one seated at table? I am among you as the one who serves" (Luke 22:26b–27).

B. "Now to him who is able to accomplish [*dýnamai poiéo*] far more [*hyperperisseúo*] than all we ask or imagine, by the power [*dýnamis*] at work [*energéo*] within us, to him be glory [*dóxa*] in the church and in Christ Jesus to all generations, forever and ever. Amen" (Eph 3:20–21).

The second pivotal image from the gospels in reference to the meaning of paradox is abundance (*perisseúo*). Encounter with Jesus is portrayed as an experience of abundance. An abundance of joy, an abundance of health and well-being, an abundance of food and drink, an abundance of fellowship, an abundance of thanksgiving (*eucharistía*), an abundance of givenness, an abundance of love. With Jesus there is more than enough (*perisseúo*) (see Matt 13:12; Luke 15:17). With Jesus comes the experience of increase, excess, and exorbitance. He is a man of poverty but somehow brings about an increase in the most desperate situations, similar to the prophet Elijah and his encounter with the widow and her son at Zarephath (see 1 Kgs 17). It is not so much a phenomenon comprised of an avaricious accumulation of goods (whether material or spiritual) but a recognition or notice of the goodness of what gives itself even in scarcity. The contemplative heart is a thankful heart. Every speck of dust becomes a treasure for contemplative perception because it gives (*es gibt*). Jesus awakens this receptivity to givenness in his witnesses: "I came so that they might have life and have it more abundantly [*perissós*]" (John 10:10).

When Jesus multiplies loaves of bread and fish for the multitude of people who come to hear him teach and witness him heal, there is an abundance left over—"more [*perisseúo*] than they could eat" (John 6:13). This abundance serves as a sign that points not to food and drink as an end in itself but to a greater meaning and purpose of food and drink: to do the will of God the Father. "I have

Paradox

food to eat of which you do not know ... My food is to do the will of the one who sent me and to finish his work ... Do not work for food that perishes but for the food that endures for eternal life, which the Son of Man will give you. For on him the Father, God, has set his seal" (John 4:32, 34; 6:27). The itinerary of Jesus does not stop on this side of eternity. Instead, he points to the possibility of eternal life in which the gift of God that has begun will continue and not cease.

Paul of Tarsus attests to this indefatigable approach of the gift. In light of Jesus's resurrection Paul writes that "this is why Christ died and came to life, that he might be Lord of both the dead and the living" (Rom 14:9). This is to say that if there is truly a Lord of heaven and earth, it stands to reason that death would not be outside the scope of this lordship. The lordship of Jesus secures the destiny of all creatures who have been welcomed into life: life. Otherwise, the lordship of Jesus would stop at death and, in effect, death would be lord over and against life and would nullify divine lordship, which, fortunately, does not make any sense. Rather, Paul exclaims, "Now to him who is able to accomplish [*dýnamai poiéo*] far more [*hyperperisseúo*] than all we ask or imagine, by the power [*dýnamis*] at work [*energéo*] within us, to him be glory [*dóxa*] in the church and in Christ Jesus to all generations, forever and ever. Amen" (Eph 3:20–21). For Paul, in view of our eschatological destiny, the abundance (*perisseúo*) attested in the gospels is redoubled into a superabundance (*hyperperisseúo*) of resurrected life in Christ. More becomes far more, abundance becomes superabundance, and life (*bíos*) becomes eternal life (*zoé aiónios*). The superabundant possibilities unlocked by divine grace give themselves according to the form of paradox (*parádoxa*) that always is accompanied by the call and response of glory (*dóxa*). This phenomenon wherein saturation itself is saturated will be taken up in the final section of the chapter.

C. "'For this reason a man shall leave his father and his mother and be joined [*davaq/proskolláomaí*] to his wife, and the two shall become one flesh.' This is a great mystery [*mystérion*], but I speak in reference to Christ and the church" (Eph 5:31–32).

A third image lifted from the Hebrew-Christian Scriptures to illuminate the meaning of paradox is that of sacrament, rooted in the primordial sacrament of marriage between one man and one woman. Pope John Paul II coined the term "theology of the body" to refer to this mysterious phenomenon in which the hidden mystery of God is manifest and proclaimed in and through the spousal meaning of the human body. Christianity is not an esoteric Gnosticism or a reductionistic materialism. What is revealed in Jesus is the goodness and beauty of the animate flesh, but an animate flesh in need of redemption. And the mystery of this redemption is made known precisely through the animate body become interpersonal gift. Marriage between a man and a woman serves as sacrament when it faithfully points to this paradoxical redemption accomplished by Christ: "'For this reason a man shall leave his father and his mother and be joined [*davaq/proskolláomai*] to his wife, and the two shall become one flesh.' This is a great mystery [*mystérion*], but I speak in reference to Christ and the church" (Eph 5:31–32). Heterosexual monogamous marriage images the union of Christ the Bridegroom and the Church the Bride. Sexual difference is a prerequisite for sexual unity. The sexual complementarity between man and woman allows for a genuine union—a union of diverse psychosomatic makeups—to take place. Sexual complementarity also is the condition of possibility for procreation and the initiation into motherhood and fatherhood. Monogamy, instead of polygamy or promiscuity, images the oneness (*ehad*) of God (see Deut 6:4). It is a paradox that two bodies become one and yet remain distinct. This union between man and woman is perfected by a mutual clinging (*davaq/proskolláomai*) to one another in the totality and reciprocity of their personhood. Just as God clings to his beloved creatures by taking on flesh in the womb of the Blessed Virgin Mary, so do husbands and wives faithfully image the mystery of salvation by clinging to one another in erotic self-donating love: "until death do us part" (see Matt 22:23–33).

The sacrament (*mystérion*) signifies the locus of salvation. It exhibits a double phenomenality inasmuch as it is a living paradox: two worlds and persons commingling together as one, one divine and the other human. The bishops of the early church used the language of *hypóstasis* to indicate the paradoxical union of natures in Jesus: one divine and the other human. Meaning either being or person, the Greek term *hypóstasis* held together the paradoxical identity of Jesus as one Person (identical to God the Son) having two natures or forms of being. The Latin theologian of Carthage, Tertullian, claimed that the flesh was the hinge of salvation because it seems entirely logical that the fullness of the divine nature would need to enter into the fallowness and lack that set in the human nature through original sin in order to redeem it. Christian faith claims a process of salvation brought about by two paradoxical unions: (1) the union of natures in the one Person of Jesus and (2) the union of two bodies in the eschatological wedding feast of the Lamb: Christ the Bridegroom and the Church the Bride. In effect, two hypostatic unions take place in two directions. As Athanasius of Alexandria and Irenaeus of Lyons put it: God became human so that humanity could become divine. It is this doubly paradoxical movement that is manifest and proclaimed in the sacraments of the church, all of which assume the pattern of the nuptial mystery of two bodies becoming one flesh.

V. PARADOX OF PARADOX

Christian faith has helped us uncover the meaning of paradox, especially as it pertains to the perennial questions we have about the prospect of salvation and eternal life. The logic of Christian faith presents an exceptionally exquisite description of the power of paradox. We observed two distinct movements within the singular movement of paradox: (1) the logic of the double negative and (2) the logic of superabundance. Yet what do these two movements have to do with one another? It is the interlocking of these two logics that forms the logic of paradox, the logic of the cross, the logic of divine love.

Paradox

First, the logic of the double negative infers a negation of negation. We notice this logic at work in speech and mathematics. The essence of the logic of the double negative is that a debt canceled is a credit earned. Even though two wrongs do not make a right, in this case, a negation of negation results in a positive outcome. Two sins are worse than one. But to sin against sin—that is, to renounce sin and to resist its logic of dissipation and destruction—is to act virtuously. In the case of language, the expression "it is not impossible" could be read, at the same time, as "it is possible." The two negations cancel one another out and the expression reads altogether as a positive statement. In mathematics, multiplication of negative numbers results in positive numbers. For example, $-8 \times -7 = 56$. In the case of this equation, it is like saying, "Removing less than seven eight times equals fifty-six." Removal of removal equals restoration. Imagine taking steps backward facing a negative direction. For example, knowing that sin signifies lack and moving away from the lack in the opposite direction. In effect, a lack of lack is fullness. Even in the wake of sin forgiveness of sin results in healing and restitution because forgiveness implies a removal of the debt, damage, and, at the limit, memory of sin. The exclusion of the impossible is possibility. There is (*es gibt*) possibility because in the beginning certainly there was not impossibility.

The logic of the double negative—the negation of negation—describes the sinful human being's movement toward God. As human beings self-enveloped in an atmosphere of sin and death, the only way out is to renounce sin and thereby to let death die. Disowning our postlapsarian condition results in divine adoption: "For those who are led by the Spirit of God are children of God. For you did not receive a spirit of slavery to fall back into fear, but you received a spirit of adoption, through which we cry, 'Abba,

Father!' The Spirit itself bears witness with our spirit that we are children of God, and if children, then heirs, heirs of God and joint heirs with Christ, if only we suffer [*páscho*] with him so that we may also be glorified [*doxázo*] with him" (Rom 8:14–17). The suffering of suffering is joy and glory because in suffering love is put to the test and suffering (*páscho*) implies its own relief and passover (*páscha*). What is revealed as eternal is life, but it is necessary for life-become-death to suffer in order to live again. Peace comes in the wake of the storm.

Second, the logic of superabundance means a saturation of saturation—abundance redoubled in the form of a shortage. Divine glory must saturate itself in divine humility and limitation in order to love into being that which is not divine—an absolutely other in relation to the transcendent immanent unified otherness of divinity. Divine self-limitation begins with the zero point of *creatio ex nihilo*, creation from nothing. Divine self-limitation continues through enduring rebellious angels and humanity all the way to incarnation, suffering, death, descending into hell, resurrection, and ascension into heaven. The entire interpersonal movement of God in relation to humanity is one of superabundant paradox. Divine glory is self-saturated in order for creatures to behold God face to face. Whereas for humanity we must accomplish the negation of our fallen nature assisted by divine grace, for divinity the unfathomable glory of divine majesty must saturate itself in order to make Godself approachable for creatures. This is precisely the phenomenality of the sacramental experience wherein the most common of elements—water, oil, light, bread, wine, bodies—become the media of divine love, porous channels of God the Holy Spirit.

The logic of superabundance—the saturation of saturation—reinstates the wonder of life and the perceptible magnitude of givenness. Yes, every speck of dust, every flower petal, every insect, every cloud, every blade of grass, every rock, every animal, every encounter, every person, every joy, every sorrow, every triumph, every trial becomes an occasion of thanksgiving (*eucharistía*) because every phenomenon is a blessed, good gift (*eu-charis-tía*) inasmuch as it gives (*es gibt*) and the divine possibility of forgiveness (*áphesis*) remains. It gives (*es gibt*) because it was given in advance (for-givenness/*Vor-gegebenheit*) and will be given in advance. The advance of the gift outruns its reception because every reception depends upon the gift to be received. "Therefore, stay awake [*gregoréo*], for you know neither the day nor the hour" (Matt 25:13). The great paradox revealed in Jesus is that the eschaton already has come. We have only to receive it in the doubly paradoxical form of love self-delimited for the sake of the limited other, under the posture of humility and the ordinary impregnated with the extraordinary—with the extra that gives order to the ordinary in the form of paradox.

Key chapter concepts: paradox, empathy, solicitude, responsibility, *fiat*, complementarity, logic of the double negative, logic of superabundance

DISCUSSION QUESTIONS

1. Define paradox and clarify why this concept is at the heart of phenomenology.
2. How is empathy a paradoxical phenomenon and how can phenomenology aid us in becoming more empathetic in our relationships?
3. Describe a paradox you have experienced in your own life and how this experience expanded your capacity for empathy.

PHENOMENOLOGY

4. Name some paradoxes indicated in the gospels. Why do you think the gospels are laced with paradox?
5. How does the logic of the double negative and superabundance function within Christian faith, as well as inspire greater possibility within our lives?

5

ETHICS

WHAT IS THE PAYOFF of contemplative phenomenology? Just and merciful ethical living. Contemplative ethics. This is to say that if we want to know what the right thing is to do and how to go about doing it, we must contemplate before acting. This is the first and most primary point. Ethical action is to be a precipitate of contemplation if it is to be an ethics that can hold water. External action always follows internal disposition, including intentionality, motivation, inspiration, conscience and the meaning toward which one strives. Ethical exteriority is determined by moral interiority. Phenomenology reveals a direct correlation between the meditations of the human heart and the machinations of human activity. Once again, phenomenology is not in the business of presenting a systematic ethics based on moral questions, but it helps point in beneficial directions. By attending to givenness phenomenology contemplates the cosmos. And by contemplating the cosmos phenomenology arrives at the most authentic ethical solutions in response to what gives itself in experience. Phenomenology unveils the formation of conscience that leads to personal and cultural ethos. It is this ethos that directs ethical action from the inside out.

Ethos precedes ethics. The heart precedes the hand. Conscience precedes conduct. Phenomenology investigates these integral relationships and fosters fidelity to what gives and how it gives. Phenomenology interprets the human person as beneficiary of givenness, as respondent to the call of the other, as agent response-able. Reception, responsibility, and giving describe the essence of the human vocation inasmuch as it gives (*es gibt*) and I, in turn, give (*Ich gebe*). For phenomenology, life unfolds as a dramatics of gift, a hermeneutics of gift, because it gives. Phenomenology is contemplation of what gives, and there is no limit to this contemplation because in the beginning, givenness, and in the end, givenness. It gives. Ethics, therefore, is composed of the responsorial to what gives. Phenomenological ethics is the responsible reception to what gives. So much contemplation, so much ethics. Phenomenological ethics does not try to manipulate what may give itself in advance. Rather, it awaits the touchdown of givenness and then contemplates its meaning. Today it seems that so many ethical programs begin with a tacit ideology, whether liberal or conservative, and then construct ethical principles and protocols from these presupposed ideologies. Phenomenology unmasks the backward and reductionistic tendencies of these proposals. Let us begin with contemplating what gives itself, call a thing what it is (as it gives), and develop our ethical frameworks accordingly.

I. ETHICS

The word *ethics* does not occur very frequently in works of phenomenology. This omission is due to the fact that phenomenology spends most of its time contemplating what gives instead of giving a detailed account of the pragmatic consequences of this contemplation. Unfortunately, this short primer on phenomenology will have to follow suit and not develop a systematic approach to ethics in miniature. Instead, the few pages to follow will distill a handful of the central ideas of Jewish phenomenologist Emmanuel Levinas (1906–95). His work undoubtedly represents the apogee of phenomenological ethics to date. In particular, formulating a post-Holocaust project in ethics as first philosophy, Levinas brings the fruits of phenomenological reflection to their highest pitch. Inspired by the proclivity for things ethical within the history of Judaism, Levinas attends to the ethical character of human experience like no other. We will follow his lead in this brief presentation of ethics as an outgrowth of contemplative phenomenology, even if the outgrowth is preceded by its own ingrowth, that is, the call of the other that predates its own recognition, contemplation, and response.

For phenomenology, ethics begins with the fundamental paradox of the person-to-person encounter: the self and the other. Phenomenology discloses an otherness outside the self and an otherness within the self, or at least makes room for this possibility. First, the other faces me from without and, second, the other calls to me from within. This twofold ethical relationship defines the uniqueness of human personhood as ethical agent par excellence. In spite of our incredible altricial and radically interdependent nature, it is self-evident that we are the most powerful creatures on earth. We have the potential to do great good for the planet and equally great evil. In a real way all creatures depend on how we live for their own life, well-being, and survival. Many biological species have become extinct at our hands. Various forms of ecological degradation occur by us at exponential rates. At the same time, new movements of ecological preservation, protection, and rejuvenation have been initiated and will help stem the tide of expedited global self-destruction. Without question we find ourselves as responsible stewards for the rest of creation.

Yet the centerpiece of this matrix is the face-to-face anthropological encounter. The care and reverence we have for one another ordains the care and reverence we have for the rest of the created order. The interpersonal encounter between the other and I is a sui generis relationship unique to persons. It consists of rationality, language, freedom—the freedom of the gift—and the limitless possibilities of interpersonal love and responsibility. Those of us who are more powerful, and who have greater capacity to give and to serve, find ourselves called all the more to responsibility for the powerless other with or without physical face. For ethics, the meaning of face is not so much an outward shape or mold as it is ethical exigency itself, the weight of the call of the other within the inner recesses of my conscious life. Even outstripping the manifest parameters of givenness, the call of the other proclaims itself as it transcends the concepts and modalities of givenness. The face appears insofar as it speaks. Levinas declares ethics as first philosophy because this phenomenology of proclamation detects a call within phenomenality that can be reduced neither to a manifestation of givenness nor to an apparition that could be situated alongside the rest. Ethics as first philosophy, even prior to a phenomenology of givenness or manifestation, responds to the non-phenomenon of the call of the other as that which generates and inspires the entire interface between the self and all phenomena that give themselves to conscious perception. Ethical exigency is a personal pre-perception that speaks an ethical meaning that makes possible and meaningful every other impersonal phenomenon.

Ethics, for phenomenology, means the face-to-face encounter between the other and me and everything this encounter entails. First comes the call of the other to me and second comes my response to her call. She need not say anything from her mouth for this call to issue itself. The call of the other is experienced primarily as a prophetic utterance of the other that wells up within the self and overflows into my verbal validation of the other who faces me: "Hello. How are you?" This is the beginning of the ethical movement toward the other—a movement that began not from my self-determination but began with the call of the other to which my response is always a rejoinder. What gives in the ethical relationship is what came before givenness, even though we inevitably must go on to describe this relationship in terms of givenness. What came before givenness is the proximity of the other and the simultaneous call of the other that surpasses even the concept of presence. Presence gives itself due to the diachronic history of the call that cannot be transposed into any givenness of the present. The call of the other proceeds from an inaccessible past that remains hidden as a past more ancient than any historical narrative could recount. Before the beginning, s/he calls.

II. ETHICS AND THE LITTLE FACE OF THE OTHER

The call of the other, which cannot be interpreted as just another episode of givenness, commences the ethical plane of phenomenology. It serves as the irreducible point of reference for all ethical discussion. This ethical basis deflects all ethical reductionisms, such as utilitarianism, proportionalism, nominalism, emotivism, social contract theory, moral relativism, or even deontological ethics as envisaged by Immanuel Kant. While not contradicting the natural law tradition and virtue ethics whatsoever, phenomenological ethics provokes ethical action not so much for the sake of the moral principle or the virtue, but for the sake of the other who faces me. I do not act virtuously in order to fulfill a precept or moral standard for its own impersonal sake. Rather, I act as a performance of my faithful response to the urgency of the call of the personal other for me to become responsible for her. In this sense my moral motivation cannot be set neatly within a closed category of metaphysics or natural law. Instead the call of the other is wild and untamed. It is unrelenting and unpredictable. It is desperate and fragile. It is without measure or volume, quality or quantity, precedence or approval. The call of the other who faces me is entirely without boundaries and beckons from beyond Cartesian coordinates that would locate its fixed point of axis. As inherently immaterial and nonspatial, the call of the other defies attempts to reduce it to an object or reproducible law of morality. The call of the other is absolute and transcends the natural order of being, though it betrays its transcendence by manifesting itself therein. As a (non-)phenomenon of spirit, the call of the other who faces me accuses me of my negligence and laxity. I have not been responsible for her enough.

Nevertheless the call continues without ceasing. It begets hope because it is never too late to ascend toward the other in responsibility for her, even in small ways. Because I am elected as agent responsible, with this responsibility signifying the fundamental meaning and destiny of my selfhood, the power of responsibility remains with me as long as I have breath in my lungs and blood pumping through my veins. These corporeal phenomena are materializations of those personal spiritual phenomena that precede them and put the material at their service to express most eloquently the meaning of self-donation and responsibility. Matter has the potential to be interpreted as the substrate through which spirit may express itself. This certainly is the meaning of the humanization or personalization of matter. The human body can serve as the bearer of the message of love, beginning with the experience of nascent life in the womb. Acceptance of responsibility of the other surely begins here as life for each of us began there. Now let us give an abbreviated phenomenological description of the call of the little face of the other in her mother's womb.

Before indicating a visually decipherable and tangible visage, the face of the other signifies the origin of my vocation to responsibility for her. The face calls before it appears. The silent gestation of the infant expresses a face that calls as ethical exigency before it appears as a naked face to the naked eye. As indwelling proximity of the other within the same, the infant in the womb—the one without voice—nevertheless speaks responsibility in me. From a biological standpoint, the infant lives from conception onward as a new eventfulness of life and unique personal givenness. Her body comes on the scene as distinct from the body of her mother and her father. Hers is a new body individuated from all other bodies and signifies interpersonal relationship from the point of conception onward. A living relationship obtains between infant and mother, infant and father, infant and the whole of society. The call of the infant is issued and seeks a responsible respondent. Her face is beyond little yet calls all the same. She calls with even greater amplitude the smaller she gives, the more hidden she gives, the more silent she gives. She gives, and even before she gives (*sie gibt*), she calls (*sie ruft an*). Her proclaimed call precedes her embodied manifestation and her body witnesses to her call. In truth, attested in her invisible call and visible givenness, she gives not mere pregnancy or problem. Rather, she gives personhood inasmuch as I give personhood, you give personhood, we give personhood. The meaning of personhood signifies call and response, individuality and relationship, created and uncreated. Since I AM (*eyeh asher eyeh, egó eimi*; see Exod 3:14), I am. Since the divine I AM envelops the womb of eternity and creation, the I am of me, a creature, gives and says itself as a response to the other who calls to me.

It is the little face of the other, as call and givenness, that provokes our contemplation on the first comer (*le premier venu*). It is this first comer who initiates the whole ethical enterprise and carries it forward. And the same can be said for the disabled face of the other, the dying face of the other, the infirm face of the other, the refugee face of the other, the immigrant face of the other, the ostracized and marginalized face of the other. Phenomenology enables us to detect those phenomena that are beyond the reach of sense perception, natural science, the objectivity of objects, the subjectivity of subjects, and even the phenomenality of givenness and manifestation that, too, must be reduced in order to make plenty good room for the other who deflects every attempt to reduce her to more of the same. Responsible interpretation of the other must go on according to the pattern of rabbinic midrash: mystery, paradox, dialectic, both/and. Phenomenology lets in fresh air to ethical questions that allegedly were decided and put to rest long ago. Phenomenological ethics helps critique the political and ideological reductionisms that want to portray ethical responsibility in some areas but not in others. Phenomenological ethics helps reawaken what the late Joseph Cardinal Bernardin called "the seamless garment of life," that is, a generous hermeneutic that is attentive to all the needs of the other under the baton of her call.

III. ETHICS IN EVERYDAY LIFE

We have considered the primacy of the face of the other, both as call and givenness, for ethics. May we apply here this hermeneutic to daily living. How can I live at the constant command of the call of the other? Is that not exhausting, relentless, impossible? If the logic of the double negative and the logic of superabundance are in force, let us entertain once again the impossibility of impossibility. Levinas, Louis-Marie Chauvet, Richard Kearney, and others have suggested the possibility of a daily liturgical tempo that is oriented around the visitation of the other: a liturgy of dailiness, a liturgy of the neighbor, an ethical life of hospitality and welcome. If we carry forward the structure of immanent phenomenality—the crossroads between call and response, givenness and hermeneutics, the phenomenon and consciousness—and link it to the level of transcendent sociality, we are led back to the Marian *fiat* of active passivity, receptive agency, responsible hospitality. Within an ethical liturgy of dailiness the call of the other is met with the response of welcome, inclusion, mercy, and self-emptying.

Flashback. I am a freshman in high school. As a budding perfectionist I struggle with many issues concerning self-esteem. I want to be the best at everything I do. The best musician in the band. The best athlete on the team. The best student in the class. I want to be recognized and noticed. I want to receive praise and honors. I want to see (and to have others see) my name in lights. If there is a record, I want to break it. If there is a goal, I want to make it. If there is a prize, I want to take it. If there is a weakness, I want to fake it. In the throes of my adolescence I interpret my self-realization as the essence of communal salvation. I am convinced that the universe orbits around me, and it would take some time for this bubble to be burst—and perhaps it reforms and then needs re-bursting again, even to this day.

It is a February Friday night in the cool of Michigan winter. The weather is almost as chilled as my soul. We have a freshman basketball game that evening at our home gymnasium. Maybe this is the night I'll score into the double-digits. Maybe this is the night I won't be afraid to shoot the ball due to the risk of missing the shot. Maybe our team will win and I will be the obvious MVP of the game. The contest proceeded against the Dowagiac Chieftains. My mother and father were in the stands to watch and cheer me on. The stupefying Barnes twins, who captivated the attention of not a few of the young men, were in the stands as well. I hardly remember anything from the game other than feeling sorely disappointed (once again) at its conclusion. We most certainly lost (again) and I am not sure if I scored into the double-digits. What I remember more vividly than anything else was slipping without notice from the gymnasium, without talking with my parents, the Barnes twins, or anyone else. I set out, without haste, to walk home in the cold by myself. I did not choose to take the safe route home. Instead, I chose to walk through a rougher part of town, but I had to cross a bridge to get there.

First I walk past the Berrien County Jail, oblivious to the prison in which I enclose myself. Then I begin to cross the bridge, staring down into the freezing waters of the St. Joseph River. Would anyone miss me if I were gone? I wish I could disappear. I'm so disappointed in myself and I'm sure the world is too. Why can't I be great? Why can't I be noticed more by other people? God, why don't you see to my greatness?

I continue along the bridge in the cold and enter the shadowy side of town. Boarded-up buildings and houses. No one in sight. Alone. I hurt. Do I want to be hurt more? Do I want other people to know how much I hurt inside? If I want people to know who I really am, why do I run from them? I continue to walk on broken sidewalks that I've never touched with my own feet before. My walk of risk and uncanniness reflects my wandering and restless heart.

I walk over a second bridge over a second river—the Paw Paw River, named after the sweet paw paw fruit. Up ahead I see a billboard advertising a local South Bend television station, WNDU 16. They relay all the latest news for the University of Notre Dame sports teams. I want to play there someday. I sense that it's my destiny. Quarterback for the University of Notre Dame Fighting Irish. Number 3. Helmets of gold. Heisman trophy. National championship. These newscasters pictured here will be announcing my name in just a few years. But our football team didn't win a game last season. My basketball team hasn't won a game this season. Crushed tonight by the Dowagiac Chieftains.

Finally I near my home, 152 Higman Park. Will my mom and dad be home? Will they be waiting for me? Will they be upset with me because they have no idea where I've been over the past several hours? It's late. It's dark. I enter the front door of my house and there is my mom sitting alone in the dark, waiting for me. She's crying and covered in a blanket. She asks me where I've been and I tell her the truth, perhaps hoping that her empathy will increase in proportion to my desperation. She is hurt and doesn't understand why I acted the way I did.

My mother, Linda (a name that means beautiful), was keeping vigil for me. She was performing her daily liturgy of responsibility for me. Through her high degree of empathy she soothed my spiritual, psychological, and somatic wounds. She continued to come to my games, whether I played much or not, and cheered me on. She was one of my greatest cheerleaders. She embodied the meaning of responsibility by adopting me, raising me, and never taking leave of the solicitude she had for me. She was my mother and she could do no other. Because she shared her very life with me, I lived. Because she listened, I spoke. Because she cried, I rejoiced. Because she died, I inherited.

Ethics

Linda perceived my call even before she saw me, touched me, held me, fed me. She welcomed me into her life once and for all as a newcomer who was, at the same time, the first comer (*le premier venu*). Because I called, she responded yes. Even though little swords would pierce her heart, like that sharp edge of a cold February Friday night, she said *fiat* in response to the call of my little face. She modeled to me a Marian Levinasian ethics long before I learned about phenomenology. She taught me the meaning of responsibility precisely by enacting it. Through mimesis, today I dare to exercise a similar posture of the greatest possibility called responsibility. Now I have six little faces who face me every day according to their intimate proximity through ordaining me as their father. Likewise I encounter the beautiful face of my bride who faces me every day according to her intimate proximity through ordaining me as her husband. Who am I? The answer to this question is bound up inside another: who are they?

Phenomenological ethics contemplates the possibilities of the heroic. Yes, the heroic in big ways and small. What would the heroic response look like in this situation or that situation? Phenomenology identifies the heroic figure as the one who sacrifices all the way to the point of abandonment. Embodied sacrifice is a love that knows no boundaries for possibility, all the way to forgiveness. For forgiveness comes as the only antidote that could devastate devastation. That which is empty can be filled only by emptying its emptiness. The hero is the one who empties emptiness by emptying himself. This is the paradox of the hero: he brings life out of death precisely by dying. Phenomenological ethics takes us beyond the demands of justice all the way to the possibilities of mercy, forgiveness, heroic sacrifice, and resurrection. It does not stop short at legalities, prescriptions, laws and litigation, but leads us to the threshold of paradoxical heroism: the law is given to the degree that it is made.

The narrative about my mother's welcome of me in the midnight hour of a desperate life features an embodied exposition of responsibility, one-for-the-other. My testimony to her solicitude itself points to its fruitfulness. The proof is in the pudding. The evidence of responsibility is in its fruit. The meaning of responsibility is brought to light in the wake of its performance and interpersonal givenness. Where there is sacrificial heroism there is life, liberty, and the pursuit of happiness. I compose this text from a land and a nation that has been fortified, despite all its lingering ambiguities, by a history inscribed with occasions of liberation, abolition, and innovation. Like so many other nations, the integrity, cohesion, and identity of the United States of America was won by sacrificial heroism. From the testimony about my mother to that of my motherland, the abstract concept of responsibility is attested in embodied sociality and solidarity: "How good and how pleasant it is, when brethren dwell together as one!" (Ps 133:1).

Following the sequence of the previous chapters of this book, we now will turn our attention to sacrificial heroism writ large, namely, Jesus of Nazareth. This is the very reason Jesus has captivated the attention of so many people over the centuries since he lived in the land of Israel. Jesus is the paradigmatic figure of sacrifice. He is the hero who lays down his life to save the rest and, paradoxically, saves his own life in the process of losing it. Instead of offering biblical exegesis of a specific text from the gospels (as done in previous chapters), the next section will contemplate the ethical life of Jesus the rabbinic phenomenologist.

IV. ETHICS AND JESUS

Jesus lived a life of sacrificial heroism. This is the testimony of the church and the reason why the church exists. The church is a herald of the proclamation of good news that God loved us into being and is loving us into redemption. This love is revealed to the maximum in Jesus, Emmanuel, God with us—a God who loves us so much that he wanted to do life with us all the way to suffering with us. Jesus's ethical life, according to a phenomenological analysis, can be characterized altogether as demonstrating the *Logos* of all logic, in a word, the logic of the cross (see 1 Cor 1:18). This is the dialectical logic of paradox, the logic of the double negative, the logic of superabundance. It is a personal logic that is manifest and proclaimed at the crossroads of the face-to-face encounter. Apart from this anthropological place of encounter, this logic is inaccessible. It is not a mathematical formula. It is not an economics of supply and demand. It is not a politics driven by the powerful wherein might is right. Rather, it is a subversive logic in which "power is made perfect in weakness" (2 Cor 12:9). This is because power made perfect in weakness is power redoubled. Power itself is one thing. But power put to the test in weakness and bringing strength to weakness exactly within the experience of weakness is a paradoxical revelation of power that surpasses the generic concept of power. The logic of the cross—certainly in reference to the saving death and resurrection of Christ—can be described according to three primary traits: alterity, humility, and love. Let us consider each of these in turn.

A. Alterity

From its Latin root, *alter*, alterity means otherness. The logic of the cross indicates a unified diversity of persons—a genuine communion of persons. It is an iconic crossing of gazes, a crossing of lives, a crossing of gift. The phenomenon of gift takes place at the intersection of self and other. Otherness is necessary for the gift to circulate, otherwise it has nowhere to go. Even those who put Jesus to death (myself included) are being loved by Jesus all the while: "Father, forgive them, they know not what they do" (Luke 23:34). The cross is intersection—the intersection of otherness. The cross expresses the encounter of otherness, always in some way suffering the other—more specifically, bearing or enduring the other as other. Admitting that I am not complete unto myself. That me, myself, and I do not form a company after all.

Alterity signifies the possibility of unity and not the other way around. Genuine unity is the result of otherness brought together as one. Not a reduction of otherness to one thing alone, but a unification of others that forms a bond of commonality and therefore a sharing of a common union or communion (*Gemeinschaft* as opposed to *Gesellschaft*). The primordial interpersonal authentication of alterity is anthropological sexual difference: male and female (see Gen 1:26-27; 2:18-25). Sexual difference communicates that an individual human being is incomplete on his or her own, by himself or herself. He does not make perfect sense without her, and she does not make complete sense without him. Anatomy and physiology point to the meaning and potential of interpersonal union as they show how masculinity is always in reference to femininity and femininity is always in reference to masculinity. Beyond (yet including) the biological teleology of procreation, our bimorphic anthropology witnesses to the universal human vocation of becoming a communion of persons in love. Otherness is required for the formation of authentic community. Otherness is a prerequisite of persons. Personhood gives itself as the relationality of alterity.

Similarly, divinity is revealed through its incarnation in Jesus as a triune unity of divine Persons. As the divine Person of the Son, Jesus reveals the essential identity and meaning of divinity as a Trinity of Love: Father, Son, and Holy Spirit. God would not be love if God were not more than one. In Jesus God gives Godself to creatures as Love. Eternal interpersonal Love. Alterity is the condition of possibility for the giving and receiving of love as gift. The ethical posture of Jesus depends on alterity and all that he says and does reinforces it. God refuses to reduce the other to more of the same and so creates a universe that is radically other than divine Otherness. Matter gives that which God gives not. Finitude gives that which God gives not. Vulnerability gives that which God gives not. Susceptibility gives that which God gives not. In other words, matter receives that which God gives. Finitude receives that which God gives. Vulnerability receives that which God gives. Susceptibility receives that which God gives.

In his interaction with so many people during his earthly sojourn, Jesus respects the otherness of the other. He does not force himself upon anyone but instead witnesses to truth and invites to belief. He testifies: "For this I was born and for this I came into the world, to testify to the truth. Everyone who belongs to the truth listens to my voice" (John 18:37). He does not reveal ultimate truth as a formula to memorize, a pill to take, or a lever to pull. This revelation is not mechanical like a puppet on a string. Divine revelation in Jesus promotes the capacity of free will to decide in favor of love or not. The paradox is that love incorporates alterity, whereas a lack of love involves alterity diminished. Hell means the lowest degree of alterity—a totalization of the self to the point of eclipsing (not annihilating completely) the beauty, truth, and goodness of interpersonal otherness. At the same time, hell means the lowest degree of unity—a totalization of the diversified other to the point of perpetually suspending the possibility of unification. What is left in the latter case is division and only division, dissension and only dissension, disintegration and only disintegration. In both cases the figure of idolatry is the same: a paradoxical totality of finitude that confuses the part for the whole, the self for the other, lust for love, vice for virtue, impossibility for possibility.

The gospel of Jesus reinstates the supreme goodness of otherness and recuperates the meaning of personhood. So much otherness, so much personhood. Personal alterity prevents the other person from being reduced to an object of use. Lust does not let the otherness of the other other itself enough. The teachings and life of Jesus, in contrast, welcome the otherness of the other as other. It is not that the teachings and life of Jesus serve to witness to the goodness of alterity, but that the goodness of alterity witnesses to the teachings and life of Jesus. Alterity is an integral element of Jesus's life and teachings and the point of this element is to point to the possibility of personal encounter and diversified union with Jesus. Alterity, in its abstract meaning, is merely a description of that face-to-face encounter between persons that comprises the givenness of salvation: eternal

B. Humility

A second core element of the logic of the cross—the logic (*logos*) of the gospel of Jesus—is humility. Humility cannot be spoken of and strived after enough, and that is its paradoxical point. To be mindful of humility and to thirst after humility is to act humbly. In this sense, the humble person never arrives at humility once and for all; otherwise he would cease to be humble. Humility includes sincere non-indifference and yet disinterestedness in relation to the other who faces me. The humble person acts with solicitude and selflessness, always in reference and deference to the other. Humility yields. Jesus exhibits this radical humility insofar as in him divinity is emptied into humanity to the point of abandonment: "He emptied himself . . . he humbled himself, becoming obedient to death, even death on a cross" (Phil 2:7–8). From its Latin roots, *humus* "ground, earth, dirt, soil, clay" and *humilitas* "lowliness, lack of stature (think of Zacchaeus!), insignificance, subservience," humility conveys the truth about humanity—a term derived from the same Latin roots as *humility*. The givenness of the meaning of human orbits around the axial meaning of humility: altricial, frail, fragile, vulnerable, susceptible, sensitive, liable, actively passive, exposed. The signature of God is written by the incarnate life of Jesus: divine humility. God becomes part of the earth (*humus*) that God made from nothing. God desires to become human because this *humus* is the most fertile medium through which to express unconditional love that at once means self-humiliating love.

PHENOMENOLOGY

In Jesus is revealed a God who not only desired to become human for the sake of humanity, to inaugurate a redemption inclusive of the entire cosmos, but also desired to self-humiliate as the best means to communicate divine love. Jesus is witnessed stooping down toward the ground often: writing in the sand to intercept the accusation of a woman caught in the act of adultery, ascending mountains only to descend them, bending low to wash his followers' feet, kneeling on the ground in the garden of Gethsemane, reclining at table with sinners become friends, permitting himself to be cast to the ground throughout his crucifixion, submitting to the earthbound supine position as he is nailed to the cross of wood, allowing his body to be laid in a tomb to rest awhile as a prelude to his resurrection. Jesus reveals a God who loves dirt, who is earthbound because this God insists on soiling the soil in order to cleanse it. This is the way in which possibility gives possibility to possibility. "Amen, amen, I say to you, unless a grain of wheat falls to the ground and dies, it remains just a grain of wheat; but if it dies, it produces much fruit" (John 12:24). The seedbed of love is humility. Divine love is manifest and proclaimed within a horticulture of humility. Humility is the measure of authentic love. Humility forgives all because it is acutely aware of the experience of received forgiveness for all: "So I tell you, her many sins have been forgiven; hence, she has shown great love. But the one to whom little is forgiven, loves little ... and forgive us our sins for we ourselves forgive everyone in debt to us" (Luke 7:47; 11:4a). Again, a sublime paradox discloses itself. Do I have much to be forgiven? If I acknowledge my many sins and failures and always bear these in mind, I grow in humility. If I deny the truth of my sinful past, I lack humility and, therefore, love little (see 1 John 1:8–10).

Humility prioritizes the life of the other and gives the other the benefit of the doubt. Humility trusts in givenness according to the paradoxical regency of receptivity and the power of possibility. Not only is divine humility on display in the incarnation of Jesus and in his saving suffering, death, and resurrection, it is attested all the more in how Jesus entrusts his message and ministry of salvation to a church composed of sinners (becoming saints). How much risk and precariousness is involved in a collaboration between divine omnipotence and human frailty! Yet divine humility does this without hesitation. This is the essence of interpersonal empowerment: to let the creative agency of the other participate fully in the holistic development of the common good. Humility resists micromanagement because it is not afraid to delegate. We witness Jesus empowering an army of witnesses become evangelists throughout the gospels. And this is the power and persuasion of the religious movement called Christianity, in spite of its ambivalent lived history between heaven and hell. A paradoxical phenomenon wherein the powerless become powerful and the powerful become powerless, the weak become strong and the strong become weak, the servants become leaders and the leaders become servants, the humble become exalted and the exalted become humble. A magnificent twist of the natural attitude and its hubris. Humility humbles the unwarranted hubris of the natural attitude and Jesus incarnates the very meaning of humility: "Take my yoke upon you and learn from me, for I am meek and humble of heart; and you will find rest for yourselves" (Matt 11:29). It is the Sacred Heart of Jesus that guides us in our perpetual contemplation of the everlasting meaning of divine humility.

C. Love

The first and final element of the logic of the cross is love, superabundant love. How could one speak of the logic of the cross without reference to love? Much like Ignatius of Loyola's prescription to contemplate love in the fourth week of his *Spiritual Exercises*, this book suggests the very same summit of truth. There is no higher reason, argument, or decisive expression of truth than authentic love because, more than anything else, it gives (*es gibt*). So much love, so much givenness. So much givenness, so much love. If the gospel of Jesus could be summed up by one word, without acting in minimalist fashion, it undoubtedly would be love. Yet we would do well to qualify or specify this love as merciful love, self-donating love, zealous love, passionate love, erotic love, kenotic love, cathartic love, responsible love, patient love, righteous love, humble love, other-centered love, solicitous love, gracious love, joyful love, beautiful love, enduring love, faithful love, hopeful love, unconditional love, eternal love, superabundant love. Who could tire of praising love? This praise marks the beginning and end (as always a new beginning) of Augustine's *Confessions*: "You are great, Lord, and highly to be praised!" (Ps 48 [47]:2). Augustine speaks not so much about God but to God, and that makes all the difference. Love, at its best, does not speak so much about the other as to the other. Theology, at its best, does not speak so much about love but to the God who is love (see 1 John 4:8, 16). So may we conclude this book with another poetics of praise that attempts to do some level of justice to the God who is love.

Indeed, you are worthy of all our praise, O LORD, God and King of the universe. You have fashioned us into being and have breathed marvelous life into us as gift. I am not worthy to address you, O God, but since you have addressed me first by creating me and by revealing yourself to us, I humbly respond to your gift of welcome by calling you *Abba*, Father. You convince me day after day that one day in your courts is better than a thousand elsewhere (see Ps 84:11). Thank you for inviting me into your courts of givenness and for the chance to be purified of my gross natural attitude not just once but many times over. I find myself in overtime because you have granted me this overtime of life to witness to your glory and to praise you in the presence of my brethren and friends. This prayer does not serve to seal everything I have written as truth but rather gives indication of my feebleness and that anything I say that is worthy of attention originally proceeds not from my own lips but yours. So may your praise ever be on my lips and may you inhabit the praises of your people (see Pss 34:1; 22:3–4). Yes, may your praise linger into the liturgical time of heaven in my mouth and on my lips and tongue. Because you touch these with your cleansing presence in the perpetual sacrifice of your altar, I shall be animated to give you praise as a responsorial to your superabundant givenness that will not go unnoticed by your creatures.

PHENOMENOLOGY

BAPTISM AT PENTECOST

You are my child I say. With you I am well pleased.
Divine humility conspires on bended knee.
YHWH-saves is my name remember donald lee.
Less is more when more is less humble feeble be.

O, my God, you alone know these bones can rise.
I alone cannot know what will be the prize.
With one word you can stir sight back to these eyes.
With all words I can blur your color, shape and size.

Fear not, friend, your time down here is not yet at an end.
Up is down and down is up exalt unwind again.
Do what is below you for to die is life on mend.
Cross and blood and pain on flood for which my Father sends.

How can I with helpless cry glorify *ha SHEM*?
Flow of blood cease tonight I touch your garment's hem.
Healing in the midnight hour joy enticing REM.
Possible for your pure power *fiat dit la femme.*

V. ETHICS INCOMPLETE

Yet for all this, ethics remains incomplete, and so does contemplation. In paradoxical fashion, this book will conclude with an admission of its inadequacy and the abiding cracks in the method of phenomenology. In the context of postmodernity, many philosophers and not a few (pseudo-) theologians have cashed out in the directions of relativism and nihilism as a reaction to the equally nefarious error of fundamentalism. But extremes meet. All reductionisms meet in the same ballpark in which there is no ball to pitch and no bat with which to hit. Without naming names suffice it to say that those who claim church doctrine as allergen misplace the origin of their sneeze. Perhaps ontotheology is not the root of all intellectual evil after all. Perhaps Dominicans and Carmelites, for instance, still have something to say to one another today. If truth is what we are after, then we must remain open to all of its varied channels. The irony of relativism is that it poses as open to all save for the absolute, and it does so absolutely! The irony of nihilism is that it claims to have found something only to have gotten lost in the process. What it has found is the alleged possibility of impossibility and in its hubris vacates the possibility of the impossibility of impossibility, namely, the possibility of letting itself be found by another (divine revelation). The irony of fundamentalism is that it claims to hold a monopoly on truth without admitting (in humility) its legion blind spots and unwarranted reductionisms. Yes indeed, if left to ourselves we perish and one moral compass is as good as the next. Yes indeed, if we pretend that we are gods and that there are many others, we drift again into the pool of Narcissus and bite into the toxic fruit of the tree of the knowledge of good and evil. Yes indeed, if truth does not circulate through the play of conversation and the conflict of interpretations, it withers up like a fig tree that bears no figs (see Mark 11:12-14). However, if we insist on our identity as seekers of truth, we may discover (because it has been shown and told to us) that truth has a face and a personal name: Jesus.

Good comprehensive phenomenology takes us to this place of encounter in which we receive the giving intuition that the *logos* of philosophy is the *Logos* of theology. Yet phenomenology lies remiss in its inability to make a definitive judgment, or even to submit its findings to a final verdict. Perhaps phenomenology is afraid that this conclusive move of its humility will disqualify its scientific genius—that it will stop play and arrest its contemplative business of description. Phenomenology resists yielding to a method not its own and granting it the last word because the good faith of phenomenology renounces the possibility of end. It perpetually resists the act of judgment as to the absolute truth or falsehood of a phenomenon. As alluded to earlier in the book, the greatest strength of phenomenology is, at the same time, its greatest weakness: indecision. And phenomenology, by itself, is unable to render a resolute decision because it lacks the necessary methodological apparatus to do so. It needs something else from somewhere else to serve the pursuit of truth all the way—to go the distance of seeking the truth, even though what phenomenology loves is the givenness of the distance itself. Paradoxically, phenomenology needs metaphysics.

Only a handful of philosophers and theologians have insisted on this twining of method over the past century: Edith Stein, Hedwig Conrad-Martius, Erich Przywara, Karl Rahner, Hans Urs von Balthasar, Paul Ricoeur, and Karol Wojtyła, to name a few. *Twining* is an appropriate term to use to refer to the dialectical proximity of method(s), as twining can imply both separation and joining together. Not a synthesis of meta-phenomenology or phenomeno-metaphysics but a dialectic between phenomenology and metaphysics. Each method must remain its own but they are called together to converse and to interact. As iron sharpens iron, so one method sharpens the other (see Prov 27:17). Phenomenological ethics results in a half-baked ethics. It bears a saturation of contemplation and inspiration but lacks an empowerment of actuality and decision. In fact, metaphysics prevents phenomenology from drifting into the ether of idealism because metaphysics secures the veracity of the real according to the exigencies of actuality, substantiality, causality and hylomorphism. Because there is (*es gibt*), it gives (*es gibt*); it gives (*es gibt*) because there is (*ipsum esse*). It will be left to another book, *Metaphysics: A Basic Introduction in a Christian Key*, to fill out what is lacking within an ironic phenomenology-limited,

Ethics

phenomenology-alone perspective. May phenomenology heed the call within the call to collaborate with metaphysics in the pursuit of truth lest it betray its missionary mandate: to the things themselves!

Key chapter concepts: ethics, ethos, ideology, exigency of responsibility, self-donation, vocation, the first comer (*le premier venu*), alterity, humility, love, communion (*Gemeinschaft*), call of the other, conscience, logic of the cross, metaphysics

DISCUSSION QUESTIONS

1. Why does phenomenology deal little with ethics?
2. How can phenomenology help establish a dynamic ethical framework for human living?
3. Recall how alterity, humility, and love secure authentic Christian ethics and how these virtues could fortify careful discernment within an ethical dilemma you face.
4. Reread the closing poem of this chapter. How might this poem apply to your own life?
5. Why is phenomenology insufficient to develop a holistic ethical framework by itself? What more is needed?

INDEX

alterity, 116–18, 127
anatomy, xv, 22, 117
angel(s), 78, 86–87, 98, 119
animal(s), 6, 8, 31, 47, 59, 84, 99
Athanasius of Alexandria, 96
atheism, 40, 69, 76
Augustine, 122

Balthasar, Hans Urs von, 126
baptism, 124
beauty, xi, 1, 5, 34, 80, 94, 118
Bernard of Clairvaux, 36
Bernardin, Joseph, 109
blood, 17, 50, 66, 107, 124
body, 22, 55, 78, 83, 85, 94, 107–8, 120

Carmelite(s), 27, 124
Catholic, 10, 53
causality, 24, 77, 126
chaos, 119
Chauvet, Louis-Marie, 110
Christian (or Christianity), 10, 20, 68, 94, 96, 100, 121, 126–27
church, 53, 56, 87, 92–96, 115, 121, 124

communion, 26, 55, 63, 74, 79, 81, 87, 116–17, 119, 127
complementarity, 94, 99
Conrad-Martius, Hedwig, 126
conscience, 54, 85, 101–2, 127
consciousness, xi, 5, 21–26, 42, 65, 110
contemplation, x–xi, xiv, 2, 14, 18, 19, 23, 25–27, 29, 31–32, 38–40, 42–43, 45, 54, 58, 65, 67, 101–3, 109, 122, 124, 126
cosmos, 26, 32, 101, 119–20

dialectic (or dialectical), xv, 12, 45, 68–73, 81, 86, 109, 115, 126
Dominican(s), 124

ego, 14, 19, 82–85
eidetic object(s), 22, 42
Einstein, Albert, 68
element(s) (or elemental), ix, 51, 74, 98, 118–19, 122

Index

empathy, 6, 38, 78–81, 84, 86, 91, 99, 112
epoché, 4, 20
es gibt, 15, 20–21, 25, 29, 32, 36, 92, 97, 99, 102, 122, 126
ethos, 38, 102, 127
evangelist, 15, 121
evangelization (or evangelism), 25, 53
evil, 76, 104, 124–25
evolutionary theory, 69
eternal, xv, 11–12, 29, 36, 56, 67, 74, 90, 93, 96, 98, 117–18, 122
evil, 76, 104, 124–25
exigency, 67, 104–5, 107, 127

Falque, Emmanuel, 55
fiat, 25, 39, 84–85, 99, 110, 113, 124
freedom, 26, 80–84, 104
fundamentalism, 44–45, 68–71, 77, 80, 124–25

geometry, 47–48
glory, xi, 32, 51, 74–75, 80, 88, 91–93, 98, 123
goodness, xiii, 15, 19, 23, 34, 41, 55, 64, 80, 92, 94, 118
gospel(s), xv–xvi, 10–11, 14–17, 33, 41, 56–57, 65, 87, 92–93, 100, 115, 118–19, 121–22
grace, vi, 5, 15, 17–18, 93, 98

Heidegger, Martin, 62, 65
hermeneutic(s), 45–46, 49–50, 71, 81–82, 102, 109–10
Holy Spirit, 39, 98, 117

Houselander, Caryll, 55
humility, xii, 33, 39, 41, 50, 56, 63–64, 91, 98–99, 116, 119–22, 124–25, 127
Husserl, Edmund, xi
hypostatic union, 96

ideology, xvi, 44, 69, 80, 102, 127
Ignatius of Loyola, 15, 122
immanent, 21–23, 42, 65, 80, 86, 98, 110
infinite, 83, 91
intellect (or intellectual), x, 28, 47, 49, 124
intelligence, x
intentionality, 17, 42, 45–48, 56, 59, 61, 63–64, 67, 71, 101
intuition, 22, 24, 38, 42, 46–48, 56, 125

jazz, xii
Jewish, 16, 32–33, 57–59, 86, 103
John Paul II, 94
Judaism, 38, 40, 68, 103

kairós, 11–12, 19–20, 63, 66–67
Kant, Immanuel, 106
Kearney, Richard, 110
kingdom of God, 12–13, 15, 20, 35–38, 57, 59, 64, 86–87

language, 19, 32, 46, 49–50, 59, 65, 95, 97, 104
le premier venu, 109, 113, 127
Levinas, Emmanuel, 65, 103–4, 110, 113

Index

liturgy, 51–52, 55, 110, 112
logic (of the cross), 89, 96, 115–16, 119, 122, 127
Logos, xii, 39, 115, 119, 125
Lonergan, Bernard, 62

Marion, Jean-Luc, v, 23, 48
marriage, 15, 87, 94
Marx, Karl, 69
Mary of Nazareth, xiii, xvi, 6, 11–12, 26, 38–43, 51, 54, 58, 64, 74, 82, 95, 101, 116
mathematics, 47–48, 69, 97
mercy, 19, 40–41, 63, 67, 110, 114
metánoia, 14, 20
metaphysics, 24, 72, 75, 77, 106, 126–27
midrash, 57–59, 70–71, 109
mind, 8, 14, 46, 52, 87, 121
morality, 73, 106
music, xii, 12, 57, 69, 76, 110
mystical, xiii, 28, 58

necessity, 53, 76
noema, 24, 42
noesis, 24, 42
nothing, 2, 7, 14, 19, 34, 36, 39, 46, 67–68, 98, 119

organism, 30

perception, xi–xiii, xvi, 4, 9, 13, 21–22, 24, 34, 40, 47, 49, 55, 59–60, 62, 65, 92, 105, 109
philosophy, xiv, 10, 29, 56, 69, 71, 103–4, 125
physiology, 22, 117
plant, 25, 30, 31
polarity, 68

pollution, ix
prayer, 27–29, 54, 71, 79, 123
Przywara, Erich, 126
pregnancy, 40, 42, 83, 108
Rahner, Karl, 126
reductionism(s), 4, 10, 17, 25, 44–45, 58, 68–71, 76, 106, 109, 124, 125
revelation, xii, xiv, 4, 10, 25, 68, 71–73, 86–87, 115, 118, 125
Ricoeur, Paul, 126
Rilke, Rainer Maria, ix

saturated, ix, 5, 46, 48, 55, 71, 91, 94, 98
self-donation, 83, 85, 91, 107, 127
sex (or sexual), 15–16, 94, 116
solicitude, 17, 38, 78–79, 81, 85–87, 99, 112, 114, 119
soul(s), ix, 14, 19, 28–29, 34, 36, 49, 54, 78–79, 85, 90, 110
space, xiii, 19, 22, 28
spirit (or spiritual/spirituality), 22, 27, 39, 61, 63, 78, 85, 92, 97–98, 107, 112, 117, 122
Stein, Edith (or Teresa Benedicta of the Cross), 126
suffering, 78, 84, 89, 98, 115–16, 121
supernatural, 40–41

Talmud (or Talmudic), 57, 71
teleology, 117
Teresa of Avila (or Teresa of Jesus), 27, 87

Index

theology, xiv–xv, 10, 29, 40, 56, 58, 68–69, 94, 123–25
Torah, 16, 58, 71
tradition(s), 10, 27, 38, 45, 47, 56–58, 65, 89, 106
transcendence, 79, 107
transcendent, 22–23, 42, 79, 80, 86, 98, 110
Trinity, 79, 87, 90, 117, 119

universal, 22–23, 83, 117

value, 5, 38, 49
vice(s), 26, 118
virtue(s), x, 26, 40, 75, 78, 106, 118, 127
vocation, 27, 37, 39, 51, 54, 83–85, 102, 107, 117, 127

wisdom, vi
Wojtyła, Karol, 126

YHWH, 61, 86, 124

www.ingramcontent.com/pod-product-compliance
Lightning Source LLC
Chambersburg PA
CBHW031501160426
43195CB00010BB/1064